America's Secret Recipes 2

RON DOUGLAS

Make Your Favorite Restaurant Dishes at Home

Special thanks to our expert "recipe cloners"

Tom Grossmann (Chef Tom)

and Marygrace Wilfrom (Kitchen Witch).

To my dear friends from The Secret Recipe Forum,

thanks for your contributions and continued support.

www.RecipeSecrets.net/forums.

PREFACE

After the huge success of *America's Secret Recipes 1*, we're back by popular demand with *America's Secret Recipes 2*.

With the help of the 65,000 members of our Secret Recipe Forum, we've tested, replicated, and compiled the recipes for 115 of the most beloved restaurant dishes in America. These are the "secret recipes" that generate billions of dollars for the restaurant industry every year. Now you can prepare them in your own kitchen!

I could go on and on about how accurate these clone recipes are, but I think one of our customers explains it best:

> "I have made MANY of the recipes, and have been thrilled EVERY time, so have all the friends and family that I have cooked for. Everybody who gets to taste my cooking says how amazing it is that these recipes taste just like the restaurants'.
>
> I was in the restaurant field for close to 4 years, and I know that everything is premade, boxed, bagged and full of blubber ready to be assembled. I love that I get the same great flavor, without the excess fat and preservatives. It's healthy, full of flavor, and I already have all of the ingredients in my kitchen.
>
> I shock myself every time I cook! I keep on wanting to compliment the cook, and then I remember that I am the cook.
>
> Thanks for helping me to realize that I love cooking!"
>
> --Martina M.

We encourage you to put the book to good use and make these famous dishes yourself. Once you've tried the recipes, you'll see what makes them so special and why we have so many satisfied customers.

You can also get thousands of additional recipes and interact with our online community through our free Secret Recipe Forum - go to: www.RecipeSecrets.net/forum.

I hope this cookbook brings enjoyment for you, your family and friends for years to come.

Ron Douglas

CONTENTS

Continued on next page

Applebee's Applebee-tini

Description: *Smirnoff twist of green apple, DeKuyper Luscious Red Apple liqueur, apple juice, and sweet and sour.*

Ingredients

1 oz DeKuyper Red Apple Liqueur®
1 oz Smirnoff Green Apple Twist®
1 oz apple juice
1 oz sour mix

1. Combine ingredients in a shaker.
2. Shake well and pour into a martini glass.

Makes 1 drink.

About Applebee's:

Applebee's® was founded in Atlanta, Georgia, by Bill and T.J. Palmer. They envisioned a restaurant that would provide full service, consistently good food, reasonable prices and quality service in a neighborhood setting. Their first restaurant, T.J. Applebee's Rx for Edibles & Elixirs®, opened in November 1980.

Applebee's Bourbon Street Steak

Description: *A juicy, tender steak with the zing of Cajun spices served with sautéed onions and mushrooms.*

Ingredients

1/2 cup bottled steak sauce
1/4 cup bourbon whiskey
1 tablespoon honey
2 teaspoons prepared mustard
2 teaspoons Cajun seasoning

4 (10-oz.) beef rib, round, or
  chuck steaks
sauteed mushrooms and onions,
  for steak topping

RecipeSecrets.net tip:
Caramelized onions are excellent for this recipe.

1. Marinate your steak: Place all ingredients (except sautéed mushrooms and onions) in a resealable plastic bag or in a glass baking dish covered with plastic wrap and place in refrigerator for at least 2 hours or overnight. Turn several times during the marinating process.
2. When ready to cook, preheat grill to medium-high heat.
3. Remove steaks from marinade and drain well; discard marinade. Season steaks on both sides with Cajun seasoning.
4. Grill steaks to desired doneness, turning halfway through grilling.
5. Serve with sautéed onions and mushrooms.

Serves 4

Applebee's Chardonnay Mushrooms

Description: *These wonderfully-flavored mushrooms are fantastic served over your favorite steak. Just the right amount of garlic, butter and Chardonnay flavor.*

Ingredients

1 lb. fresh mushrooms, quartered
1/2 cup fresh butter
1/2 teaspoon salt
1/4 teaspoon black pepper
1/4 teaspoon granulated or powdered garlic
1/4 cup Chardonnay
dried parsley flakes

1. Wash mushrooms under cold running water; drain. Cut mushrooms into quarters.
2. Melt butter in saucepan over low heat; add mushrooms and season to taste with salt, pepper and garlic. Increase heat to medium and cook, stirring often, until soft, approximately 4 minutes.
3. Turn off heat and immediately pour Chardonnay over mushrooms. Add parsley and toss to coat. Serve over steak.

Serves 4

RecipeSecrets.net tip:
These can be prepared ahead of time and refrigerated with a loose cover over them. If mushrooms do not cool completely in 4 hours — discard — do not serve.

Applebee's Classic Patty Melt

Description: *A tasty seasoned burger grilled to perfection, served on butter-grilled bread and topped with sauteed onions and melted cheeses.*

Ingredients

2 burger patties
salt, pepper, garlic powder, to
  taste
melted butter, as needed
4 pieces Italian bread
4 tablespoons mayonnaise
  blended with roasted garlic
  and mustard
4 slices Swiss cheese

4 slices Cheddar cheese
1 cup sliced onions

1. Season burger with salt, pepper and garlic and place seasoned side down on grill or in broiler. Season top side of burger. Cook to desired doneness, flipping halfway through grilling.
2. Meanwhile, melt butter in skillet over medium heat. Spread mayonnaise on one side of bread slices. Place bread slices in skillet to brown with the mayonnaise side up. Move the bread slices around in the pan to coat with the melted butter.
3. Place Swiss cheese on one slice of mayonnaise-coated bread, and Cheddar on the other.
4. In separate skillet, melt butter and saute onions, seasoning to taste with salt, pepper and garlic.
5. Transfer cooked patties to one slice of bread and the sautéed onions to the other. Carefully assemble and cut in half. Serve.

Serves 2

Applebee's Crispy Orange Chicken Bowl

Description: *Delicately spiced breaded chicken covered in a spicy-sweet orange glaze and served over almond rice pilaf and a tasty mix of mushrooms, broccoli, red peppers, sugar snap peas and shredded carrots. Topped with toasted almonds and crispy noodles.*

Ingredients

Chicken:
1 egg
1 1/2 teaspoons salt
1/4 teaspoon pepper
1 tablespoon vegetable oil
2 lbs boneless skinless chicken
1/2 cup plus 1 tablespoon
  cornstarch
1/4 cup all-purpose flour
oil, for frying

Vegetables:
1 1/2 cups broccoli florets
1 cup sliced red bell pepper
3/4 cup sugar snap or snow
  peas
1/4 cup shredded carrot
1 cup sliced mushrooms
  (optional)

Glaze:
1 cup orange juice
1/2 cup light brown sugar, firmly
  packed
3 tablespoons orange
  marmalade

2 tablespoons soy sauce
1 tablespoon vegetable oil
1/2 teaspoon minced parsley
1/4 teaspoon chili flakes
1/4 teaspoon minced garlic
1/8 teaspoon dried thyme
1 tablespoon rice wine vinegar

Almond Rice Pilaf:
3 tablespoons butter
1/4 cup diced onions
1/4 cup celery
1 cup uncooked converted rice
2 1/4 cups chicken broth
1/8 teaspoon salt
1 teaspoon dried parsley
1/3 cup slivered almonds

Topping:
1/2 cup crispy chow mein
  noodles
1/4 cup slivered almonds

1. Prepare chicken: In bowl, combine egg, salt, pepper and oil; mix well. Set aside.

2. Cut chicken into 2-inch pieces; add to egg mixture; stir well; set aside.

3. In separate bowl, combine cornstarch and flour; mix well. Add chicken; stir to coat each piece well.

4. Heat ½-inch oil in wok or heavy skillet over high heat (to temperature of 375 degrees F.). Carefully add chicken in small batches and fry 3 to 5 minutes or until golden and crisp. (Do not overcook - it will toughen the chicken.) Remove with slotted spoon and drain on paper towels.

5. Prepare rice pilaf: Heat butter, saute onions and celery until tender — do not brown. Add rice and cook 2 to 3 minutes, stirring with a wooden spoon; do not brown — just until the rice turns opaque. Add chicken broth, salt and parsley; bring to boil; cover; reduce heat to low; cook without stirring 12 to 15 minutes or until all the chicken broth has been absorbed. Stir in almonds.

6. Meanwhile, steam vegetables until crisp-tender.

7. Prepare glaze: In skillet used for frying chicken, remove all but 2 tablespoons of the oil and reduce heat to medium. Saute garlic (if the oil is too hot your garlic with have a bitter taste); add remaining ingredients; bring to boil, stirring constantly; reduce heat and simmer to thicken to desired consistency.

8. To serve, toss chicken and vegetables in glaze and serve over a bed of rice pilaf; top with slivered almonds and crispy noodles.

Serves 4-6

RecipeSecrets.net tip: Save time: Grab a bag of Chinese-style vegetables from your grocer's freezer case.

A&W BBQ Beef Sandwiches

Description: *Serve this zesty roast beef filling on your favorite hamburger buns.*

Ingredients

4 cups shredded cooked beef roast or round steak
1 cup Heinz ketchup
1 cup apple butter
1 cup Catalina dressing
1/4 cup Heinz 57 sauce
2 tablespoons Worcestershire sauce

1. Using a 2 ½-quart baking dish, combine all ingredients and mix well. Cover tightly.
2. Place in preheated 375 degree F. oven for 45 minutes or until piping hot.
3. This will fill 8 hamburger buns. Serve hot.

Serves 4

About A&W Restaurants:

A&W Restaurants® are distinguished by their draft root beer, as well as their burgers, hotdogs and fries. They started in business back in 1919, in Lodi, California by Roy Allen and Frank Wright — thus the name A&W.

B.B. King's Blues Club and Restaurant Barbecued Ribs

Description: *These dry-rubbed and BBQ sauce slathered ribs have that distinctive flavor that has made B.B. King famous.*

Ingredients

2 lbs. pork loin ribs
Dry Spice Rub (page 10)
4 cups canned tomato sauce
1/2 cup diced tomatoes
1/4 cup firmly packed brown
  sugar

1/4 tablespoon Worcestershire
  sauce
2 tablespoons dried onion
1/4 cup soy sauce
1/4 cup water

RecipeSecrets.net tip:
Serve with coleslaw and grilled corn on the cob.

1. Prepare Dry Spice Rub (recipe on page 10). Using your fingers, sprinkle the rub over ribs and rub in well; repeat on other side. Place ribs in baking dish and cover with plastic wrap. Place in refrigerator for 4 to 6 hours to marinate.

2. Over very low heat, in saucepan, combine tomato sauce, tomatoes, brown sugar, Worcestershire sauce, onion, soy sauce and water. Add 1/2 cup Dry Spice Rub and blend well; cover. Cook 3 hours.

3. To cook ribs: Preheat grill or smoker to low. Place ribs on grill and cook, covered, 3 to 5 hours. Brush with sauce during the last minutes of cooking.

4. Serve ribs with the remaining sauce.

Serves 2

About B.B. King's Blues Club & Restaurant:

B.B. King's® Blues Club & Restaurant is a cross between the nightclub experience and a nice restaurant. It's a great place to get dinner and hear some great music.

B.B. King's Blues Club and Restaurant Dry Spice Rub

Description: *This rub adds great flavor to your ribs.*

Ingredients

1 cup chili powder
1 tablespoon garlic granules
1 teaspoon onion powder
1/2 teaspoon cumin
1 1/2 teaspoons salt
2 tablespoons seasoned salt

1. Combine all ingredients; blend well.
2. Transfer to airtight container and store in dry place.

RecipeSecrets.net tip:
This rub is very good on pork chops and steaks.

Bahama Breeze Fish in a Bag

Description: *These moist and tasty mahi mahi fillets are served over tasty vegetables.*

Ingredients

2 sheets parchment paper
2 fresh mahi-mahi fillets
1 teaspoon Adobo seasoning
1/4 teaspoon ground annatto seed
Vegetable Saute (page 13)
4 slices vine ripened tomato
4 sprigs fresh thyme

1. Preheat oven to 350 degrees F.
2. Prepare "bags" for fish. Fold a piece of parchment paper in half to make a rectangular shape that is 13 X 18 inches. Cut into a half-circle using kitchen shears. Once unfolded, it should be a full circle. Repeat for the second fillet.
3. Using a sharp fillet knife, slice each mahi fillet diagonally on the bias making 3 pieces of equal size.
4. In small bowl, combine Adobo and ground annatto seed (both available in Latin markets) and sprinkle over both sides of mahi fillets.
5. Begin layering: Unfold parchment and place 2 tablespoons Vegetable Saute on one half of the circle; top with a mahi fillet; top fillet with 4 tablespoons Vegetable Saute and place a slice of tomato on top. Place your second fillet on top of tomato and spoon more Vegetable Saute on top, another tomato slice and top it with the 3rd mahi fillet. Spoon more Vegetable Saute on top and add fresh thyme sprigs. Repeat with other mahi fillets on the second piece of parchment.

RecipeSecrets.net tip: Serve with black beans and yellow rice.

6. Finish making "bags": Bring the remaining side of the parchment over the fish and vegetable layers and begin to seal the edges. Crimp and fold in ½-inch deep and 2-inch wide folds all the way around. Carefully place bags on baking sheet and place in middle of preheated oven. Bake for 18 to 20 minutes. When done, the paper pouch will puff from the steam trapped inside. Carefully unroll an edge (it will be steaming hot) and insert a meat thermometer into the center of a fillet. It should read 150 to 155 degrees F. when done.

Serves 2

About Bahama Breeze:

Bahama Breeze® is an American restaurant specializing in Caribbean-inspired fresh seafood, chicken and steaks. Founded in Orlando, Florida, in 1996, there are over 2 dozen locations throughout the states.

Bahama Breeze Vegetable Saute

Description: *A great side dish for your favorite entree.*

Ingredients

2 teaspoons extra-virgin olive oil
1 large clove garlic, minced
1/2 red bell pepper, julienned
1/2 yellow bell pepper, julienned
1/2 green bell pepper, julienned
1/2 chayote squash, seeded and
  sliced
1 stick celery, sliced
1/4 cup chicken broth

8 mushrooms, sliced
1 teaspoon chopped fresh thyme
1/4 teaspoon white pepper
2 tablespoons dry white wine
1/2 teaspoon salt

1. In large skillet over high heat, heat oil. Add vegetables and saute until softened, stirring often.
2. Reduce heat to low; add remaining ingredients.
3. Stirring often, cook for 2 more minutes; remove from heat. Cool slightly before using.

RecipeSecrets.net tip: Substitute any summer squash, such as yellow squash or zucchini for chayote in this recipe.

Serves 2

Balducci's Portobello, Spinach, and Goat Cheese Lasagna

Description: *A perfect lasagna with a medley of spinach, shallots, Portobello mushrooms and cheeses giving it an unforgettably wonderful flavor.*

Ingredients

2/3 cup olive oil, divided use
2 shallots, minced fine
2 cloves garlic, peeled and minced fine
2 lbs. Portobello mushrooms, stems removed, wiped clean, and sliced
1/3 cup dry white wine
2 tablespoons chopped fresh basil
1 tablespoon chopped fresh thyme

1 1/2 cups fresh ricotta cheese
2 cups grated mozzarella cheese
salt and pepper to taste
1 lb fresh baby spinach, rinsed and well drained
12 oz soft goat cheese (chevre), divided use
1/3 teaspoon fresh grated nutmeg
1 lb dried lasagna noodles, cooked and drained

1. Preheat oven to 350 degrees F. Spray 11 X 9-inch baking pan with non-stick spray; set aside.
2. In large saucepan, heat 1/3 cup olive oil. Add shallots and garlic; saute until tender, about 2 minutes. Add mushrooms; saute another 4 to 5 minutes; stir frequently.
3. Pour wine around the edge of the pan to deglaze; simmer until liquid has almost evaporated.
4. Remove from heat; add herbs, ricotta and half the grated mozzarella; season with salt and pepper to taste; set aside.
5. In large skillet, heat remaining 1/3 cup olive oil; add spinach and saute until tender, about 2 to 3 minutes.
6. Transfer spinach to colander and drain, pressing with the back of a spoon or spatula to remove the excess

water. Transfer drained spinach to large bowl; add remaining mozzarella and half the goat cheese; sprinkle with the nutmeg and stir until mixture is creamy.

7. Spread 1/3 mushroom mixture over prepared baking dish; top with a layer of pasta; spoon ½ the spinach mixture over.

8. Continue to layer in baking dish - pasta, mushrooms, pasta, spinach. Finish with a layer of mushrooms and top with remaining goat cheese. Cover with foil.

9. Place baking dish in preheated oven and bake for 35 minutes or until heated through. Remove foil and continue to bake an additional 10 to 15 minutes, until cheese has browned and is bubbling. Allow to rest for 10 minutes before cutting.

Serves: 10

About Balducci's:

Balducci's® is a unique market with restaurant-quality prepared foods. They currently have 10 stores on the U.S. East Coast.

Bennigan's Baked Monte Cristo Sandwich

Description: *A stacked sandwich of turkey and Swiss, baked and not fried. Served with a Dijon mustard dipping sauce.*

Ingredients

4 (1 oz.) slices Swiss cheese
4 (1 oz.) slices cooked turkey
8 slices firm white bread
3 eggs
2/3 cup milk
1 envelope dry onion soup mix
3 tablespoons butter or
   margarine

Dijon Mustard Dipping Sauce:
1/2 cup sour cream
2 tablespoons milk
1 tablespoon Dijon mustard

1. Preheat oven to 450 degrees F.
2. Place 1 slice of cheese and 1 slice of turkey on each of 4 bread slices. Top each with a slice of bread to make 4 sandwiches.
3. In pie plate beat eggs, milk and dry soup mix until well blended. Dip each sandwich into egg mixture, spooning onion pieces onto bread.
4. Make sure all egg mixture is used. Place butter in 15 x 10-inch jelly roll pan. Set in oven a couple of minutes to melt butter.
5. Carefully place sandwiches in pan and drizzle any remaining egg mixture over them. Bake 5 minutes. Carefully turn sandwiches and continue baking until golden brown.
6. Prepare dipping sauce: In bowl, combine the sour cream, milk and mustard. Mix well and then chill until ready to serve.

Serves 4

About Bennigan's:

Bennigan's got started in 1976 and was one of the earliest theme based chains of casual dining restaurants here in the U.S. They were famous for their fried mozzarella sticks, Monte Cristo Sandwiches and other tasty, but often fatty, treats. Bennigan's Irish-themed restaurants had a great ambiance, at least in the early days.

Bisquick Pancake & Baking Mix

Description: *Make your own homemade version of Bisquick for all your baking needs.*

Ingredients

8 cups flour
1 1/4 cups nonfat dry milk powder
1/4 cup baking powder
1 tablespoon salt
2 cups shortening

1. In a very large bowl, combine flour, milk powder, baking powder, and salt and mix.
2. Cut in shortening until it resembles coarse cornmeal. Store in tightly closed covered container in a cool place.

Makes about 10 cups.

About Bisquick:

Baking mixes are standard these days, but Bisquick was a revolutionary product in 1931. Never before had a pre-mixed baking mix appeared on grocery shelves. Consumers loved it, and Bisquick remains the category leader today.

Black-Eyed Pea Broccoli-Cheese Soup

Description: *Tender cuts of broccoli smothered in a creamy cheese broth.*

Ingredients

1 1/2 lbs. fresh broccoli
2 cups water
1 lb. Velveeta Pasteurized Cheese Spread
3/4 teaspoon salt
1/2 teaspoon pepper
1/2 cup cornstarch mixed with 1 cup cold water
1 pint half-and-half

1. Steam or boil (and drain) broccoli until tender.
2. Place 2 cups of water and half and half in top of double boiler. Add cheese; season to taste with salt and pepper. Stir frequently until cheese has melted; add broccoli.
3. In small bowl, combine cornstarch and water; stir to combine. Add to cheese mixture; heat over simmering water until soup thickens, stirring.

Serves: 4

About Black-Eyed Pea:

Black-Eyed Pea® was founded in 1975 by Gene Street in Dallas, Texas, and eventually expanded across the southern United States. Their menu features home-style Southern cuisine - catfish, chicken fried steak, mashed potatoes, fried okra, cornbread and rolls along with their signature dish, black-eyed peas.

Bob Evans Maple Sausage Breakfast Burritos

Description: *A fluffy omelet filled with crumbled sausage, peppers, onions, and cheeses — wrapped in a flour tortilla — served with salsa.*

Ingredients

10 (10-inch) flour tortillas
1 (1 lb.) package Bob Evans Maple Sausage
1/2 cup diced red or green pepper
8 eggs, lightly beaten
1/4 cup thinly sliced green onion
1/2 cup cream cheese spread, room temperature
1/2 cup grated Monterey Jack cheese
1 cup salsa, to serve

1. Heat tortillas: Wrap in foil and place in 300 degree F. oven to warm.
2. Meanwhile, in large skillet over medium heat, brown crumbled sausage and pepper. When sausage has browned, pour in beaten eggs and onion; cook, stirring, to cook through.
3. Combine softened cream cheese with Monterey Jack cheese and spread a thin layer of cheese mixture over each heated tortilla. Top with sausage mixture and roll. Serve with salsa.

Serves: 10

About Bob Evans:

Bob Evans began making sausage on his southeastern Ohio farm to serve at a 12-stool diner he owned in nearby Gallipolis in 1948. Made from the hogs he raised, he used all the best parts of the hog, including the hams and tenderloin.

Brown Derby Old-Fashioned French Dressing

Description: *A Brown Derby original with just the right "zing" adding a great flavor to their famous Cobb Salad. Also goes very well on your favorite salads and makes a tasty dressing for those chicken/veggie and cheese sandwiches.*

Ingredients

1 cup water
1 cup red wine vinegar
1 teaspoon sugar
juice of 1/2 lemon
2 1/2 teaspoons salt
1 teaspoon ground black pepper

1 teaspoon Worcestershire sauce
1 teaspoon English mustard
1 clove garlic, chopped
1 cup olive oil
3 cups salad (vegetable) oil

1. In large bowl, combine all ingredients except oils. Blend well; add oils and mix well. Transfer to a large jar with cover and refrigerate.
2. Shake well before using. This dressing will keep well in the refrigerator.

Makes about 1 1/2 quarts.

About Brown Derby:

The very first Brown Derby Restaurant was generally referred to as the Wilshire Brown Derby, located on Wilshire Blvd. in Los Angeles, California. Opened by Herbert Somborn and Bob Cobb back in the 1930s, by 1941 the Brown Derby was considered more famous than any movie star, according to newspaper accounts. But their famous Cobb Salad and French Dressing recipes are still here for us to enjoy.

Brown Derby Original Cobb Salad

Description: *Recreate this famous Brown Derby salad of crisp greens layered with rows of chives, tomatoes, chicken, bacon, avocado, eggs and cheese. Served with their famous French dressing.*

Ingredients

1/2 head romaine
1/2 head of lettuce
1/2 bunch watercress
1 small bunch chicory
2 medium tomatoes, seeded
2 chicken breasts, boiled
6 strips crisp bacon
1 avocado
3 hard-cooked eggs, chopped

2 tablespoons chopped chives
1/2 cup crumbled imported
  Roquefort cheese
1 cup Brown Derby Old-
  Fashioned French Dressing
  (see page 21)

1. Using a sharp knife, finely cut lettuces, watercress and chicory; transfer to salad bowl. Halve tomatoes and remove seeds; dice small and sprinkle over greens.
2. Dice chicken breasts and arrange over diced tomatoes. Top with finely chopped bacon.
3. Cut avocado into small pieces and arrange around the edge of the salad bowl. Sprinkle salad with chopped eggs, chopped chives and crumbled cheese.
4. Just before serving toss with French dressing.

Serves: 4 to 6

California Pizza Kitchen Basic Pizza Dough

Description: *Make your own pizza dough - also good for making stromboli, calzones, bread sticks, pizza rolls and fried dough - even a loaf of bread or homemade rolls.*

Ingredients

1 teaspoon yeast
1/2 cup plus 1 tablespoon warm water (105 to 110 degrees F)
1 1/2 cups bread flour or all-purpose flour
2 teaspoons granulated sugar
1 teaspoon salt
1 tablespoon extra-virgin olive oil plus 1 teaspoon for coating

To Make The Dough:

1. Proof yeast: Stir yeast into warm water; set aside for 15 minutes. Be careful with the water temperature - 120 degrees F. and above is too hot and will kill the yeast, preventing your dough from rising.

2. Prepare dough: If you are using an electric stand mixer to mix your dough, use your mixing paddle attachment. The dough hook will not work for a batch of dough this size. Add remaining ingredients (except the additional teaspoon olive oil) with dissolved yeast in mixing bowl. Do not pour the salt directly into the yeast water - that too can kill some of the yeast. Using the lowest speeds, mix gradually, for 2 to 3 minutes, or until the dough is smooth and elastic. Be careful not to over mix or your dough will rise too fast. If using a food processor: Using a plastic blade, follow instructions as written above.

Mix only until a smooth ball of dough has formed. If mixing by hand: Place dry ingredients in large mixing bowl. Make a well in the center and pour in liquids (still reserving the additional teaspoon olive oil). Combine ingredients using a wooden spoon. When dough is ready, place on lightly floured surface and knead for 5 minutes. Dough should be slightly sticky - not sticking to your hands.

3. Drizzle a bit of oil in a large bowl; place ball of dough in bowl, turning to coat lightly with oil; cover tightly with plastic wrap. Let rise in warm spot - free from drafts - until double in bulk, about 1 ½ to 2 hours.

4. Punch down dough; once again form into a ball and return to bowl. Cover again with plastic wrap and place in refrigerator, overnight, undisturbed.

5. If using for making bread or rolls you can form into loaf, sticks or rolls and place on baking sheet; cover and place in warm spot free from drafts and allow to rise for 45 minutes to an hour. Bake in preheated 350 degree F. oven until golden.

6. About 2 hours before assembling pizza, remove dough from refrigerator and using a sharp knife, divide into 2 equal portions (or 4 if making four 6-inch pizzas).

7. Roll portions of dough into round balls on a smooth clean surface. Seal any holes by pinching or rolling.

8. Transfer balls of dough to a glass casserole dish, allowing enough room for each to double in size. Seal top of dish airtight with plastic wrap. Allow to sit at room temperature until double in size - about 2 hours.

RecipeSecrets.net tip: This dough can be used as you would any bread dough recipe.

To stretch and form the dough for pizza:

1. Sprinkle a dusting of flour over a clean, smooth surface. Carefully remove a ball of dough keeping its
   round shape. Flour dough liberally.
2. Using hands, press dough down forming a flat circle
   (you can use your rolling pin if you want) about ½-
   inch thick. Continue to stretch outward until you
   have a dough that is 9-inches in diameter. Make an
   edge about ¼-inch higher than the surface of the
   dough by pinching the dough with your fingers to
   form the edge.

To dress the pizza:

1. Sprinkle cornmeal lightly over a wooden pizza peel if
   using a peel and a pizza stone. If not, use baking
   sheets or pizza pans that have been lightly greased
   or sprayed with non-stick spray. Dress pizzas and
   bake until done. If using a peel, work quickly or the
   dough will become soggy or sticky. Place toppings
   on dough.
2. If using a peel and a pizza stone (which should be
   preheating in your oven) transfer pizza from peel to
   stone. To be sure pizza releases from peel give it a
   small test jerk. If the dough does not move freely,
   carefully lift the edges of the dough and try to rotate
   it by hand. You may have to sprinkle addition flour
   under the edges of the pizza. Position the edge of
   the peel over the center of the stone about 2/3 from
   the front of the stone. Tilt the peel to start the pizza
   sliding off; once the pizza touches the stone, pull the
   peel quickly from under it. Don't move the pizza on
   the stone until it has started to set and has baked for
   at least 3 minutes. Then the peel can easily be slid
   under the pizza to move it.
3. Bake pizzas in preheated 450 degree F. oven until
   done. Check bottom of crust by carefully lifting to
   check for doneness. Carefully remove from oven to

large cutting board or dish to serve (depending on size of pizza).

Makes dough for two 9-inch pizzas.

About California Pizza Kitchen:

California Pizza Kitchen® opened in 1985. All of their innovative pizzas are creatively designed and hearth-baked to perfection.

California Pizza Kitchen Tuscan Hummus

Description: *This zesty hummus goes very well with toasted pita bread.*

Ingredients

10 medium garlic cloves
30 oz can canned cannellini
 beans, drained
1/2 cup sesame paste (tahini)
1/4 cup freshly squeezed lemon
 juice
1/4 cup olive oil
1 tablespoon plus 1/2 teaspoon
 soy sauce

1 1/2 teaspoons salt
1 1/2 teaspoons ground cumin
1/8 teaspoon ground coriander
1/2 teaspoon cayenne pepper
1/4-1/2 cup cold water, if
 needed
2 tablespoons minced fresh
 Italian parsley

1. Place garlic cloves in food processor, pulsing to mince. Scrape down sides of bowl if needed between pulses.
2. Add beans and continue to pulse until coarsely chopped.
3. With processor running, slowly pour sesame paste through tube and puree mixture.
4. Continue running processor and pour in lemon juice, olive oil and soy sauce. Stop the processor occasionally to scrape down the sides of the bowl.
5. Add salt, cumin, coriander and cayenne; process until thoroughly blended. If too thick, add ¼ to ½ cup water.
6. Transfer mixture to bowl; cover; refrigerate before serving.
7. When ready to serve, preheat oven to 250 degrees F. Place pita breads on baking sheet and heat until thoroughly warmed, about 6 to 8 minutes.

8. Remove from oven, sprinkle with chopped parsley and carefully cut into wedges. Serve with chilled hummus.

Serves 6

RecipeSecrets.net tip:
Cannellini beans (Italian beans) are similar to Navy Beans and Great Northern Beans.

Carrabba's Italian Grill House Salad Dressing

Description: *A creamy dressing for your favorite salads.*

Ingredients

1/2 cup mayonnaise
1/4 cup grated Parmesan cheese
1/4 cup buttermilk
1/4 teaspoon minced garlic
1/2 teaspoon minced fresh parsley
1/2 teaspoon lemon juice

RecipeSecrets.net tip:
This also makes a nice
dipping sauce for chicken
fingers.

1. In small bowl, combine all ingredients, mixing well.
2. Transfer to covered container and store in refrigerator. Shake well before using.

Makes 1 cup.

About Carrabba's Italian Grill:

Carrabba's Italian Grill® was founded by Johnny Carrabba and Damian Mandola in December of 1986. Many of the recipes on their menu are those of Damian's mother Grace and sister Rose. Damian preserved the Italian authenticity of Carrabba's food by traveling the world in search of unique Italian dishes and by taking numerous trips to his grandparents' native Italy.

The Cheesecake Factory Bang-Bang Chicken & Shrimp

Description: *A spicy Thai dish flavored with curry, chile and coconut, sauteed with vegetables and served on a bed of rice.*

Ingredients

2 chicken breast fillets
16 large raw shrimp, shelled
1/4 cup cornstarch
1/2 cup vegetable oil
4 cups cooked white rice

3 cups coconut milk
2 medium carrots, julienned
1 small zucchini, julienned
1/2 cup frozen peas

Curry Sauce:
2 teaspoons chili oil
1/4 cup onion
2 tablespoons minced garlic
  cloves
2 teaspoons ginger
1 cup chicken broth
1/2 teaspoon ground cumin
1/2 teaspoon ground coriander
1/2 teaspoon paprika
1/4 teaspoon salt
1/4 teaspoon ground black
  pepper
1/4 teaspoon ground mace
1/4 teaspoon turmeric

Peanut Sauce:
1/4 cup creamy peanut butter
2 tablespoons water
4 teaspoons sugar
1 tablespoon soy sauce
1 teaspoon rice vinegar
1 teaspoon lime juice
1/2 teaspoon chili oil

Garnish:
1 1/2 cups flaked coconut
1/2 teaspoon dried parsley,
  crumbled
2 tablespoons chopped peanuts
2 green onions, julienned

1. Prepare curry sauce: In large saucepan heat chili oil over medium heat; when hot, add onion, garlic and ginger; saute for 30 seconds; add chicken broth and spices; stir well to combine. Simmer 5 minutes; add coconut milk and bring to boil; reduce heat; simmer until sauce begins to thicken, about 20 minutes. Add carrots and zucchini; add frozen peas; simmer an additional 10 minutes or until carrots become tender.

2. Prepare peanut sauce: In small saucepan, combine peanut butter, water, sugar, soy sauce, lime juice, rice vinegar and chili oil; place over medium heat. Stir to combine. Just as mixture begins to bubble, cover pan and remove from heat.

3. Meanwhile, preheat oven to 300 degrees F. Spread flaked coconut on baking sheet and toast in preheated oven, stirring every 10 minutes until evenly browned. This should take about 20 to 25 minutes. Watch carefully, you do not want it to brown too much. Remove from oven and allow to cool.

4. With sharp knife, cut chicken breasts into bite-sized pieces. Coat diced chicken and shrimp with cornstarch. In large skillet or wok, heat vegetable oil over medium heat. When oil is hot, add coated chicken; saute, stirring, for a few minutes to cook. Add shrimp and continue to cook for several minutes, until chicken and shrimp are cooked through. Remove to paper towels to drain.

5. Divide into portions (2 or 4) by filling soup bowls with hot, cooked rice, pressing down in bowl. Invert bowl onto center of serving plate, tap a bit to loosen and lift bowl. You should have a pile of rice in the center of each plate. Equally divide chicken and shrimp, spooning around rice. Spoon curry sauce and vegetables over the chicken and shrimp, be careful not to get any sauce on top of the rice.

6. Lightly spoon peanut sauce over the dish, mostly over the rice.

7. Sprinkle parsley over center of rice; top with 2 tablespoons of chopped peanuts and place a pile of julienned green onions over top. Sprinkle chicken and shrimp with toasted coconut. Serve hot.

Serves 4

Chi Chi's Sweet Corn Cake

Description: *Perfect as a side dish but sweet enough for dessert. The corn-flavor goes especially well with chicken dishes.*

Ingredients

1/2 cup (1 stick butter),
  softened
1/3 cup masa harina
1/4 cup water
1 1/2 cups frozen corn, thawed
1/4 cup cornmeal
1/3 cup sugar
2 tablespoons heavy cream
1/4 teaspoon salt

1/2 teaspoon baking powder

RecipeSecrets.net tip:
Masa harina is a Mexican corn flour. It can be found in the Spanish section at your grocery store.

1. Preheat oven to 350 degrees F.
2. Place butter in medium bowl and using electric mixer, beat well until creamy.
3. Add masa harina and water; continue beating until well combined.
4. Place corn in blender or food processor and pulse to coarsely chop, leaving several pieces of corn whole. Add to creamed mixture and stir to combine.
5. Add cornmeal and stir to combine.
6. In separate bowls combine sugar, cream, salt and baking powder; whisk until well blended.
7. Using a wooden spoon, combine both mixtures; mix well.
8. Pour into ungreased 8 x 8-inch baking pan and cover with aluminum foil.
9. Place this pan into a 13 X 9-inch baking pan. Add hot

water to pan (do not pour over 8 x 8-inch pan) to measure about 1/3 up the sides of the pan. Bake for 50-60 minutes or until the corn cake is cooked through. When the corn cake is done, remove the small pan from the larger pan and let sit for at least 10 minutes. Carefully discard the hot water from the larger baking pan.

10. To serve, scoop out each portion with an ice cream scoop or rounded spoon.

Serves 4

About Chi Chi's:

Since 1976, Chi Chi's restaurants have been known for their fun atmosphere and great Mexican-style food.

Chi Chi's Seafood Enchiladas

Description: *These easy-to-make enchiladas make a great lunch, dinner or snack. A wonderful blend of crab, cheese and onions topped with cream of chicken soup.*

Ingredients

1 (10-oz.) can cream of chicken soup, undiluted
1/2 cup onions; chopped
dash nutmeg
dash pepper
hot pepper sauce (optional)
8 oz crab meat; chopped
1 3/4 cups shredded Monterey Jack cheese, divided use
8 (5- to 6-inch) flour tortillas
1 cup milk

1. In a mixing bowl stir together soup, onion, nutmeg and black pepper. Add a dash of hot pepper sauce to soup mix if desired.
2. In another bowl, place half of the soup mixture, crab, and 1 cup of the Monterey jack cheese; set aside. Wrap the tortillas in paper towels; microwave on 100% power for 30-60 seconds.
3. Place 1/3 cup mixture on each tortilla; roll up. Place seam side down in a greased 12 x 7 1/2 dish. Stir milk into the reserved soup mixture, pour over enchiladas.
4. Microwave, covered, on high for 12-14 minutes. Sprinkle with the remaining cheese. Let stand for 10 minutes.

Serves 8

Chick-Fil-A Chicken Sandwich

Description: *Lightly breaded and seasoned, skinless, boneless chicken topped with dill pickle and served on a steamed bun.*

Ingredients

3 cups peanut oil
1 egg
1 cup milk
1 cup flour
2 1/2 tablespoons powdered
  sugar
1/2 teaspoon pepper
2 tablespoons salt
2 skinless, boneless chicken
  breasts, halved

4 plain hamburger buns
2 tablespoons melted butter
8 dill pickle slices

1. Heat the peanut oil in a pressure cooker to about 400 degrees F.
2. In small bowl, whisk egg; whisk in milk.
3. In separate bowl, combine flour, sugar, pepper and salt; whisk to combine.
4. Dip each piece of chicken in milk to fully moisten; transfer to flour mixture and pressing with fingers, coat both sides well.
5. Place chicken in hot oil; close pressure cooker. When steam starts shooting through the pressure release, set the timer for 3-½ minutes. *Important: Do not close steam release. It is very dangerous.*
6. Meanwhile, spread a coating of melted butter on the face of each bun. Place two pickle slices on heel of each bun.
7. Remove cooked chicken from cooker; drain on paper towels. Place on heel of bun. To make a deluxe chicken sandwich, simply add two tomato slices and a leaf of lettuce. Mayonnaise or bleu cheese dressing

also goes well on this sandwich. Assemble sandwich and serve.

Serves 4

About Chick-Fil-A:

In 1946 The Dwarf Grill opened and in 1964 they invented the original chicken sandwich. Its popularity brought about the opening of the first mall location of Chick-Fil-A® in 1967. In 1982 they were the first chain to sell chicken nuggets nationally. In 1986 they opened their first free-standing restaurant. They now have expanded their menu and they have over 1,000 locations.

Chipotle's Mexican Grill Cilantro-Lime Rice

Description: *Fluffy rice with a hint of citrus and cilantro.*

Ingredients

1 teaspoon vegetable oil
2/3 cup white basmati rice, uncooked
juice from one lime
1 cup water
½ teaspoon salt
2 teaspoons fresh chopped cilantro

1. In a heavy 2-quart saucepan, heat the vegetable oil over low heat.
2. Add rice and lime juice, stir for 1 minute.
3. Add water and salt, and then bring to a full boil.
4. Once boiling, cover; reduce heat to low and simmer for about 25 minutes. The water should be completely absorbed.
5. Fluff the rice with a fork and serve.

Serves 2

About Chipotle Mexican Grill:

The first Chipotle Mexican Grill opened near the University of Denver in 1993. Their unique motto of "Food With Integrity" focuses on using ingredients that are unprocessed, family-farmed, sustainable, nutritious, naturally raised, added hormone free, organic, and artisanal. McDonald's had owned a majority stake in Chipotle in the past but sold their stake when Chipotle became a public corporation in 2006.

Chipotle's Mexican Grill Guacamole

Description: *The perfect blend of avocados and onions with the kick of jalapeno and a hint of citrus.*

Ingredients

2 ripe Haas avocados
1 teaspoon fresh lemon juice
1 teaspoon fresh lime juice
¼ cup red onion, chopped small
2 tablespoons chopped fresh cilantro
2 cloves garlic, minced
¼ teaspoon salt
½ Serrano chili, seeded and chopped
tortilla chips, to serve

1. Slice the avocado in half and remove the pit. Use a spoon to scoop the avocado into a bowl. Mash the avocado with a fork leaving some small chunks.
2. Add lemon and lime juice, then mix lightly.
3. Add the remaining ingredients and stir together.
4. Serve with tortilla chips.

Serves 4-6

Claim Jumper Raspberry Swirl White Chocolate Cheesecake

Description: *A decadent, raspberry-swirled, white chocolate filled cheesecake. Makes a great dessert or rewarding treat.*

Ingredients

Crust:
9-oz. pkg. vanilla wafer cookies, finely crushed
1/4 cup butter, melted
1/4 cup packed brown sugar

Filling:
4-oz. white chocolate (such as Lindt brand), chopped
3 (8-oz.) packages cream cheese, softened

1 cup sugar
1 cup sour cream
3 eggs
2 tablespoons lemon juice
3 tablespoons flour
2 teaspoons vanilla
12-oz. can raspberry dessert filling

1. Preheat oven to 325°F.
2. Prepare crust: In medium bowl, combine cookie crumbs, butter and brown sugar. Press firmly on bottom and sides of a 9" spring form pan.
3. Prepare filling: Melt white chocolate in top of double boiler over simmering water until smooth, stirring often. Remove from over water.
4. In large bowl, beat cheese until fluffy. Beat in melted white chocolate, sugar, sour cream and eggs until smooth. On low speed, add lemon juice, flour and vanilla; mix well.
5. In medium bowl, stir one-third of the batter into strained raspberry filling. Mix well.
6. Pour remaining batter into prepared pan; using spoon, drop the raspberry filling into the plain batter. With knife, swirl filling into batter.

7. Bake 1 hour or until center is set. Cool slightly

8. Carefully loosen top of cheesecake from the edge of pan with a tip of a sharp knife. Cool and chill. Remove sides of pan. Garnish as desired. This cheesecake tastes best when refrigerated overnight before serving.

Serves 8

About Claim Jumper:

Claim Jumper® is famous for their large portions of comfort foods. First opened in 1977, and has close to 50 restaurants to date. Their extensive menu is popular with everyone — from children to seniors.

Cracker Barrel Baked Macaroni & Cheese

Description: *An old-fashioned mac and cheese recipe that is sure to become a family favorite. Real cheese and real good!*

Ingredients

2 tablespoons butter
2 tablespoons flour
1 teaspoon salt
1 teaspoon dry mustard
2 1/2 cups milk

2 cups Cheddar (8 oz.), divided
2 cups elbow macaroni (8 oz.)
1/4 cup buttered bread crumbs
paprika

1. Butter a 2-quart casserole; set aside. Preheat oven to 375 degrees F.
2. In medium saucepan, melt butter. Whisking, add flour, salt and mustard; add milk and whisk constantly until sauce thickens a little. Do not boil milk. Add 1 ½ cups cheese, heat until melted, stirring constantly. Remove from heat.
3. Meanwhile, cook macaroni as directed; drain well; do not rinse.
4. Toss macaroni with cheese sauce, coating well; transfer to prepared casserole dish; top with remaining cheese; and sprinkle with a dusting of paprika.
5. Bake in preheated oven for 20 to 25 minutes or until heated through, bubbly and nicely browned.

Serves 4-6

About Cracker Barrel:

Cracker Barrel® opened in 1969, serving good ol' country cookin' to their customers. Their cornbread comes from cornmeal, not a mix; mashed potatoes are made from real potatoes; and scratch biscuits come with real butter.

Cracker Barrel Chicken Salad

Description: *An old-time chicken salad made with chunks of chicken breast served on a bed of lettuce surrounded with cheese, tomato and egg.*

Ingredients

2 lbs. chicken breasts
2 ribs celery, cut in chunks
2 chicken bouillon cubes
2 (3-oz.) cans chunk chicken;
  shredded fine
2 tablespoons dill pickle relish
2 tablespoons finely diced onion
1/4 cup finely minced celery
2/3 cup mayonnaise

1/3 cup sour cream
2 tablespoons Miracle Whip
  Salad Dressing
lettuce, torn
Cheddar cheese wedges
1 tomato, quartered
hard-boiled egg halves
extra dressing

1. Place chicken breast in saucepan; add celery chunks and bouillon cubes. Add cold water to cover and cook until tender. Remove from broth; refrigerate until very cold. (This is a great make-ahead dish or even a good way to use leftover chicken.) Discard broth.

2. Dice cold chicken into bite-sized pieces. Transfer to large bowl and add canned chicken, relish, onion, and celery.

3. In small bowl, combine mayonnaise, sour cream and Miracle Whip; blend well. Pour over chicken mixture and mix well.

4. To serve: Using an ice cream scoop, place a scoop of salad on lettuce leaves and surround with cheese, tomato and egg. Serve immediately.

Serves 6-8

Cracker Barrel Grilled Chicken Tenderloin

Description: *Chicken marinated in Italian dressing with a hint of citrus and grilled until golden.*

Ingredients

1/2 cup Italian dressing (strain and discard spices)
1 teaspoon fresh lime juice
1 1/2 teaspoons honey
1 lb. chicken breast tenders

RecipeSecrets.net tip: Steak or turkey also works well with this recipe.

1. In small bowl, combine dressing, lime juice and honey; mix well.

2. Place chicken tenders in glass baking dish in single layer and pour marinade over; turn to coat. Cover and refrigerate for 1 hour, turning tenders after 30 minutes.

3. When ready to cook, prepare grill. Grill tenders until lightly golden in color and cooked through. Be careful not to overcook or they will dry out.

Serves 4-6

Cracker Jacks

Description: *A good old-fashioned blend of popcorn and nuts, drizzled with caramel.*

Ingredients

4 quarts popped popcorn
1 cup peanuts
4 tablespoons butter
1 cup brown sugar, firmly packed
1/2 cup light corn syrup
2 tablespoons molasses
1/4 teaspoon salt

1. Preheat the oven to 250° F.
2. Place popcorn and peanuts on baking sheets in single layer; place in preheated oven.
3. In saucepan, combine remaining ingredients. Place over medium heat and bring to boil, stirring. Using a candy thermometer, bring mixture to hard-crack stage (290 degrees F., or to the point at which the syrup forms a hard but pliable ball when dripped into cold water). This should take about 20 to 25 minutes. Your mixture will be turning darker brown.
4. After 25 minues, remove baking sheets from oven. Working quickly, pour caramel in a fine stream over popcorn and peanuts; return sheets to oven and bake for 10 minutes. Stir well after 5 minutes to coat all popcorn and peanuts.
5. Remove from oven and cool. Store in covered container when completely cold.

About Cracker Jacks:

A German immigrant named Frederick William Rueckheim invented Cracker Jacks. He came to Chicago in 1872 to help clean up after the famous Chicago fire. He also worked selling popcorn from a cart; after experimenting with a delightful popcorn candy, he started to mass produce it.

Dan Marino's Penne Portobello Pasta

Description: *Penne pasta topped with mozzarella and sliced grilled portobello mushrooms.*

Ingredients

Garlic Butter:
1/4 cup soft butter
2 large garlic cloves, minced

Penne, Mushrooms and Mozzarella:
1/3 cup dry white wine
1 tablespoon lemon juice
1 tablespoon minced garlic
1 tablespoon butter
1 (3 1/2-inch diameter) portobello mushroom
1 tablespoon olive oil

1 (4 oz.) fresh mozzarella ball, cut into 4 slices
8 oz. dried penne pasta, cooked al dente
1 medium-ripe tomato, seeded and diced
3 tablespoons chopped fresh basil
1/2 teaspoon kosher salt, or to taste
1/2 teaspoon coarse-ground black pepper, or to taste
chopped fresh parsley, for garnish

1. To make butter: Combine butter and garlic, mix well; set aside.
2. To make penne: In a nonreactive skillet or saute pan, stir together white wine, lemon juice, garlic and butter.
3. Preheat broiler element of your oven. Remove stem and scrape away gills from the mushroom cap. Discard stem and gills. Brush both sides of mushroom cap with olive oil. Place on a small broiler pan and broil 4 to 5 inches from heat source about 2 minutes a side, or until just cooked through.
4. Remove from oven and let cool to room temperature. Diagonally slice cap into 4 equal slices. Spread mushrooms on broiler pan and top with mozzarella slices; set aside.

RecipeSecrets.net tip: Portobello, or Baby Bella mushrooms really add a great flavor to this dish.

5. Bring white wine mixture to a boil over medium heat. Add cooked penne pasta to this sauce and toss to heat through. Toss in tomatoes, basil, salt and pepper and return to boil. Stir in Garlic Butter and toss again to coat well. Keep hot over very low heat while you finish mushrooms and cheese.

6. With broiler again preheated, slide broiler pan under heat source 40 seconds, just long enough to melt cheese. Divide pasta between two warm serving bowls and slide half mushrooms and cheese over top of each. Garnish with parsley.

Serves 2

About Dan Marino's:

This Hall of Fame quarterback from the Miami Dolphins opened two restaurants in South Florida, which feature creative and detailed menus from appetizers to desserts.

Dave and Buster's Cajun Shrimp Alfredo

Description: *Blackened-seasoned shrimp sauteed with mushrooms and garlic in a cream sauce served over pasta.*

Ingredients

10 oz. large shrimp, peeled and de-veined
2 to 3 tablespoons plus Paul Prudhommes Blackened Poultry Magic, divided use
3 tablespoons olive oil
1 1/2 cups chopped mushrooms
2 teaspoons fresh minced garlic
3/4 cup diced tomatoes
1 cup heavy cream

1 cup freshly grated Romano, Asiago or Parmesan cheese
1 egg yolk
1/2 cup chopped green onions
8 oz. fresh linguine or fettuccine

1. Bring large pot of water to boil; add pasta and cook al dente (to the bite). Drain; do not rinse.
2. Meanwhile, toss shrimp in 1 tablespoon Blackened Poultry Magic Seasoning.
3. In heavy skillet, heat olive oil; add seasoned shrimp and saute for about 1 minute, or until the shrimp colors, turning several times during the cooking process.
4. Add mushrooms and continue to cook for several minutes. Add garlic and tomatoes, continue stirring, and saute for a few seconds.
5. Add cream and 1 to 2 tablespoons (to taste) Blackened Poultry Magic Seasoning; bring to simmer - but do not boil cream.
6. Add cheese, egg yolk and green onions; toss over medium heat until sauce thickens — but do not boil. Control your heat source — too high a heat and your eggs will curdle and look scrambled.
7. Place drained pasta in serving bowl and pour sauce

over. Toss lightly to coat.
8. Serve with focaccia or garlic bread and extra cheese for topping, if desired.

Serves 2

About Dave & Buster's:

In the late 70's in Little Rock, Arkansas, there were two businesses next door to each other. A man named Buster ran a casual restaurant and a man named Dave ran "Slick Willy's World of Entertainment."

The two men eventually became friends and noticed that patrons would be seen going from one business to the other. That inspired them to combine their businesses and create Dave and Busters — a fun place to eat, play games, and have a good time.

Denny's Chicken Fajita Breakfast Skillet

Description: *A nice breakfast or brunch dish made with chicken, home fries and cheese. Served with sour cream, guacamole and salsa.*

Ingredients

2 boneless skinless chicken
   breast halves
1 teaspoon Fajita seasoning
1 small onion
1 small bell pepper
2 cups cooked home fries or
   hash browns
salt and pepper

4 eggs
1/4 cup half and half
1/2 cup shredded cheese
1/2 cup sour cream (optional)
1/2 cup guacamole (optional)
salsa (optional)

1. Rub chicken breast with Fajita seasoning and let marinate for 1/2 hour.
2. Slice marinated chicken into strips.
3. Spray heavy skillet with non-stick cooking spray; place chicken in hot skillet and braise until done.
4. Increase heat to high and add onion and pepper; stir fry until cooked through (you want to cook these quickly). Remove from heat.
5. Brown leftover cooked potatoes or use frozen hash browns, cooked to desired crispness. Salt and pepper to taste.
6. Divide potatoes between two serving platters.
7. Combine eggs with half and half; season with salt and pepper to taste. Cook egg mixture as two separate omelets. Place on top of browned potatoes.
8. Divide Fajita meat, and onions and peppers equally between the two platters, placing on top of omelet. Divide cheese and sprinkle over top. Serve with sour

cream, guacamole, and salsa if you like.

Serves 2

About Denny's:

The restaurant chain that we know as Denny's®
began in Lakewood, Calif. in 1953 with a dream and
a donut stand called Danny's Donuts. In 1959,
Danny's was renamed Denny's to avoid confusion
with another small chain in Southern California called
"Coffee Dan's." Doughnuts were phased out and the
menu grew to include sandwiches and other entrees.

Dreamland BBQ Sauce

Description: *The perfect sauce for your ribs! Just the right kick with added sweetness makes this secret sauce a real keeper.*

Ingredients

1 (28 oz.) can tomato puree
1/3 cup yellow mustard
3 cups water
1 1/2 cups cider vinegar
1/4 cup dark corn syrup
2 tablespoons lemon juice
1 tablespoon granulated sugar
1 tablespoon brown sugar
2 tablespoons chili powder

1 tablespoon dry mustard
1 tablespoon paprika
2 teaspoons cayenne pepper
2 teaspoons onion powder
1 teaspoon salt
1 teaspoon black pepper,
  coarsely ground
1/2 teaspoon garlic powder

1. In medium saucepan over medium-high heat, whisk together tomato puree and mustard until smooth; stir in remaining ingredients; bring to boil.
2. Once sauce comes to a boil, reduce heat and simmer for 30 minutes. Serve sauce warm.

Makes about 2 cups.

About Dreamland:

After years of toiling as a mason, John Bishop dreamed of opening his own cafe. His dreams soon became a reality. It was 1958 when "Big Daddy" John Bishop opened his first Dreamland Café. In the beginning Big Daddy had an extensive menu — but it was his ribs and secret sauce that has made him famous.

El Torito Black Bean Soup

Description: *A healthy and delicious chicken-based black bean soup with carrots and celery - and a slight kick.*

Ingredients

12 oz. dried black beans
8 cups chicken or vegetable
  stock
2 teaspoons olive oil
1 onion, chopped
1 cup chopped carrots
1 cup chopped celery
2 cloves garlic, minced
2 teaspoons dried oregano

1 teaspoon dried thyme
1 bay leaf
1/2 teaspoon cayenne pepper
salt and pepper, to taste
3 tablespoons fresh lime juice
fresh cilantro (optional)

RecipeSecrets.net tip: If you are not a fan of cilantro - just substitute parsley.

1. Sort through beans, discarding any that are shriveled or discolored; rinse thoroughly. Place in large stock pot, cover with water; place in refrigerator to soak overnight.

2. The next day, drain beans and return to pot; add stock; heat to boiling.

3. Meanwhile, in large skillet over medium-high heat, saute onion, carrot, celery and garlic in hot oil until tender, about 5 minutes. Transfer to pot; add oregano, thyme, bay leaf and cayenne pepper. Bring to simmer, cover, reduce heat and allow to simmer for 3 to 4 hours.

4. Transfer soup to blender in batches and puree to desired thickness.

5. Just before serving, adjust seasoning with salt and pepper to taste. Add lime juice and garnish with a sprig of fresh cilantro.

Serves 4

About El Torito:

El Torito® Sports Bar opened in 1982 serving flavorful, succulent, meaty pork ribs, peel-your-own shrimp and tangy BBQ chicken as well as many other favorites.

Famous Dave's BBQ Sauce

Description: *Make this famous BBQ sauce right in your own kitchen. Sweet, spicy, and citrus flavored.*

Ingredients

2 slices hickory-smoked bacon (thick cut strips)
1/3 cup chopped vidalia onion or other sweet onion
1/4 cup water
3/4 cup Peach Schnapps
1/2 cup baking raisins
1 large jalapeno pepper, finely diced
2 garlic cloves, minced
1/3 cup aged Alessi Balsamic vinegar
1/4 cup frozen tangerine juice concentrate
1/4 cup frozen pineapple concentrate
3 tablespoons molasses
2 tablespoons apple cider vinegar
2 tablespoons fresh lemon juice
2 tablespoons fresh lime juice

2 1/4 cups dark corn syrup
1 (12 oz.) can tomato paste
1/2 cup packed light brown sugar
1/2 cup Worcestershire sauce
2 tablespoons prepared mustard
2 teaspoons chili powder
1 teaspoon Maggi Seasoning
1 teaspoon salt
1/2 teaspoon crushed red pepper flakes
1/4 teaspoon fresh coarse ground black pepper
1 teaspoon cayenne
1/4 cup Kahlua
1 teaspoon liquid smoke

1. Place bacon in large skillet and fry until crisp; drain; reserve 1 tablespoon of the drippings in skillet.

2. Add onions to skillet and over medium-high heat caramelize until a dark golden brown. Be careful not to burn; reduce heat to medium low and deglaze pan with water.

3. Stir in schnapps, raisins, jalapeno and garlic; simmer 10 minutes or until mixture has a syrupy consistency; stir occasionally to prevent sticking.

RecipeSecrets.net tip:
You can substitute regular raisins in this recipe. Just soak in hot water to plump; drain to use.

4. Remove from heat and transfer to blender (you may have to do it in batches) and add vinegars, juice concentrates, molasses, lemon and lime juices. Puree and return to saucepan.

5. To saucepan, add corn syrup, tomato paste, brown sugar, Worcestershire sauce, mustard, chili powder, Maggi Seasoning, salt, red pepper flakes, black pepper and cayenne. Mix well and bring to low boil over medium heat; stir frequently.

6. Reduce heat to low; simmer 20 minutes, stirring occasionally.

7. Remove from heat; stir in Kahlua and liquid smoke. Cool, and transfer to glass bottle; place in refrigerator. When completely cold, cover. Store in refrigerator.

About Famous Dave's:

Dave Anderson, founder of Famous Dave's opened his first restaurant in Wisconsin in 1994. Dave is a BBQ legend known for having smoked tons of ribs in an old garbage can. That same garbage can is now part of his theme restaurant decor. He perfected his system to smoke good "que" by first hand rubbing each slab with a blend of southern spices, then slow smoking 'em in a pit of smoldering hickory. This became the traditional way used by champion pit-masters down in the deep south.

Famous Dave's Jumpin', Juken' & Jiven All Day Beef Brisket and Secret Moppin' Sauce

Description: Use the Famous Dave's BBQ Sauce recipe on page 55 as the base for the moppin' sauce. Garlic and rib rub for your brisket and a tasty moppin' sauce to top it all off.

Ingredients

Secret Moppin' Sauce:
3 (20-oz.) bottles
  Famous Dave's BBQ sauce
2 quarts water
1 cup beef stock base
1/4 cup Kahlua
2 tablespoons yellow mustard
2 tablespoons blackstrap
  molasses
1 tablespoon liquid smoke
1 teaspoon toasted sesame seed
  oil

1 teaspoon coarse ground black
  pepper
1/2 teaspoon crushed red
  pepper flakes
2 sticks (1 cup) butter

Beef:
whole brisket
1 tablespoon fresh minced garlic
1/2 cup rib rub

1. When purchasing your brisket, ask your butcher to remove most of the fat from the whole brisket, leaving about ¼-inch to preserve juiciness during the cooking process. Also, have him separate the brisket into two muscles, the flat and the point.

2. To prepare sauce, place all ingredients in stockpot; mix well; cook over medium-high heat and bring to simmer; reduce heat; simmer 20 minutes, stirring occasionally.

3. Using your fingers massage the rib rub into all sides of the meat; let sit for 30 minutes for the flavors to be absorbed.

4. Set your smoker to 200 degrees F. Place briskets in smoker and smoke for 8 hours. Keep the temperature of the smoker at 200 degrees F.

5. After 4 hours of smoking, beginning mopping with sauce every hour. After 8 hours of smoking, the briskets should be almost black. That is the combination of the smoke, rib rub and the sauce. You will have a crunchy "bark" exterior.

6. Place briskets on a double layer of aluminum foil, pour 2 cups of Moppin' Sauce over and seal foil tightly. Return briskets to grill (at 200 degrees F.) and continue to grill for 3 hours.

7. Remove briskets from foil; allow to cool completely. Wrap in plastic wrap; refrigerate overnight.

8. When ready to serve the next day, place back in smoker, over indirect heat at 225 to 235 degrees F. for 2 to 3 hours or until the internal temperature reaches 160 degrees F.

9. Let stand 15 minutes before slicing. By slicing just before serving, your briskets will remain juicy.

Serves: 12 - 16

Four Seasons Crab Cakes

Description: *A combination of lump crabmeat and fresh cod fillet combined with a fine blend of seasonings.*

Ingredients

2 lbs. jumbo lump crabmeat
1/2 lb. fresh codfish fillet
1/2 to 1 cup heavy cream
1 tablespoon Dijon mustard
2 teaspoons sesame oil
2 tablespoons finely chopped
  parsley

2 tablespoons finely chopped chives
2 tablespoons basil, julienned
salt and pepper to taste
juice of 1/2 lemon
olive oil for sautéing

1. Remove shells from crabmeat, picking through, being careful not to break up the large lumps of crabmeat too much; set aside.
2. Place cod fish in food processor and puree; add ½ cup heavy cream; puree until incorporated. If needed, add additional cream. This mixture should be smooth and shiny, but firm enough to hold its shape.
3. Transfer to metal bowl; add remaining ingredients except for olive oil. Preheat oven to 450 degrees F.
4. Heat oil in heavy skillet. Place a small portion of mixture in pan and saute until golden brown; taste to adjust seasoning.
5. Form mixture into crab cakes and saute in hot oil until golden brown on both sides. Transfer cakes to baking sheet and place in preheated oven to finish cooking, 4 to 5 minutes.

Serves 6-8

About Four Seasons:

Four Seasons is one of the most popular restaurants in New York City and is a hot spot for tourists. It's known for its celebrity clientele and delicious cuisine. Chef Christian Albin's award-winning menu of American seasonal specialties was created from locally grown ingredients.

Gardenburger

Description: *Gardenburgers are the original veggie burgers made with real, natural ingredients.*

Ingredients

2 tablespoons bulgur wheat
1/2 cup oatmeal (rolled oats)
2/3 cup cooked, cooled brown
  rice
1 lb. fresh mushrooms,
  halved or quartered
1 cup diced onion
1/2 cup shredded low-fat
  mozzarella cheese
2 tablespoons shredded low-fat
  Cheddar cheese

2 tablespoons low-fat cottage
  cheese
1/2 teaspoon salt
1/2 teaspoon garlic powder
1 dash pepper
2 tablespoons cornstarch

1. In small bowl, combine wheat and ¼ cup boiling water; mix well and set aside until wheat has doubled in size, approximately 1 hour.

2. In small bowl, soak oats in ½ cup water for 10 minutes.

3. In small saucepan add a little water, saute mushrooms until tender, about 5 to 7 minutes, transfer to bowl; add onions to same pan with a little water and saute until tender; transfer to separate bowl.

4. When ready, drain excess water from wheat and from oats. Transfer wheat, oats, mushrooms, rice, cheeses and seasoning to food processor; pulse until finely chopped but not pureed, about 4 or 5 times.

5. Transfer mixture to bowl; add onions and cornstarch; mix well.

6. Preheat oven to 300 degrees F. Spray large skillet with cooking oil; place over medium-high heat.

7. Using ½ cup measure, shape into patties about ½-

inch thick. Brown on each side; remove from frying pan to lightly sprayed baking sheet.

8. Bake 22 to 25 minutes in preheated oven, turn patties halfway through baking time. Remove from baking sheet and allow to cool completely.

9. When completely cold, wrap patties and place in resealable freezer bags. Freeze.

Serves 4

RecipeSecrets.net tip:
These burgers are perfect for vegetarians.

Golden Corral Bourbon Chicken

Description: *Marinated chicken in a whiskey-wine sauce.*

Ingredients

1 lb. chicken leg or thigh
  meat, cut into bite-sized
  chunks
4 oz. soy sauce
1/2 cup firmly packed brown
  sugar

1/2 teaspoon garlic powder
1 teaspoon powdered ginger
2 tablespoons dried minced
  onion
1/2 cup Jim Beam Bourbon
  Whiskey

1. Place chicken pieces in medium bowl. In small bowl, combine soy sauce brown sugar, garlic powder, ginger, onion and whiskey and mix well; pour over chicken; stir. Cover and refrigerate for several hours, stirring occasionally.

2. When ready to bake, preheat oven to 350 degrees F. Transfer chicken pieces to baking dish in single layer. Pour marinade over. Bake for one hour, basting every 10 minutes.

3. When cooked through, remove chicken from pan; scrape up pan juices with brown bits and transfer to frying pan; heat through. Add wine.

4. Stirring, add chicken and heat through for 5 minutes. Serve hot.

Serves 4

About Golden Corral:

Golden Corral® is a family-style restaurant chain that features a large buffet and grill offering numerous hot and cold items, a carving station and their Brass Bell Bakery.

Hard Rock Cafe Cheeseburgers

Description: *A mildly seasoned burger topped with cheese, sauteed onions, and served on a grilled bun; served with a side of fries and lettuce, onions, tomatoes and bean sprouts on the side.*

Ingredients

Hard Rock Cafe Seasoning Salt
  (see page 66)
2 hamburger patties
salt and pepper, to taste
2 slices your favorite cheese
vegetable oil for deep frying
pre-cut, frozen French fry
  potatoes
2 hamburger buns
lettuce, to taste
red onion rings, to taste

tomato slices, 1/4-inch-thick, to
  taste
pickles, 1/4-inch-thick, to taste
1 yellow onion, 1/2-inch-thick
  slices
1 cup bean sprouts
2 tablespoons melted butter

1. Prepare Hard Rock Café Seasoning Salt (recipe on page 66).

2. Prepare grill. Place patties on grill, season top side with Hard Rock Cafe Seasoning Salt and cook to desired doneness, seasoning the other side after flipping burgers. Top with cheese slices, if desired.

3. Meanwhile, in a large cast-iron Dutch oven, heat oil for deep frying to 350 to 365 degrees F. Carefully drop fries into hot oil. To prevent splattering caused by ice crystals on frozen fries, remove fries from freezer and allow to thaw a bit causing ice crystals to melt; shake off excess moisture. Cook fries until golden; drain on paper towels; sprinkle with Seasoning Salt to taste.

4. Brush insides of split buns with melted butter and place butter side down and toast.

RecipeSecrets.net tip:
For a healthy alternative, try using ground chicken or turkey for your burgers.

5. Assemble burgers: Heel of bun, burger, sautéed onions, crown of bun. Arrange fries next to burger. Garnish with lettuce, tomato slices and bean sprouts. Serve immediately.

Serves 2

About Hard Rock Cafe:

Hard Rock Cafe® is known throughout the world - owning the world's greatest collection of music memorabilia which they display in all their locations. The first Hard Rock Cafe opened its doors to the public in 1971 in London, England.

Hard Rock Cafe Love Me Tenders with Sauce

Description: *Mildly seasoned, breaded chicken strips fried until golden and served with a honey mustard sauce.*

Ingredients

1 egg
1/4 cup milk
2 lbs. chicken tenderloins
1/2 cup all-purpose flour
1/2 cup seasoned bread crumbs
vegetable oil for frying

Sauce:
1 cup yellow mustard
1/2 cup honey
1/4 cup mayonnaise

1. Make sauce: In small bowl, combine sauce ingredients and blend well; refrigerate, covered, until ready to serve.
2. In medium bowl, combine egg and milk; mix well. Roll chicken strips in flour, coating evenly. Dip flour-coated strips in egg mixture, drain off excess and roll in crumbs, pressing to coat evenly.
3. Place on plate and allow to sit for 15 minutes.
4. Meanwhile, heat oil in deep fryer to 350 degrees F. Deep fry for several minutes until cooked through and golden brown. You may have to do this in batches. Drain on paper towels. Serve immediately with sauce.

Serves 8

Hard Rock Cafe Seasoning Salt

Description: *A blend of seasonings that will complement burgers, chicken, steaks, pork, seafood, vegetable dishes, soups, stews and casseroles.*

Ingredients

1/2 cup kosher salt
1 1/2 teaspoons granulated onion
1 1/2 teaspoons granulated garlic
1 1/2 teaspoons coarse black pepper
1 1/2 teaspoons celery salt

RecipeSecrets.net tip:
This seasoning can be used on meat, poultry, fish or any veggie dish.

1. In small bowl, combine all ingredients; mix thoroughly.

2. Store airtight in pantry. This can be used in any recipe calling for seasoning salt.

Makes about 1/2 cup.

Houlihan's Baked Potato Soup

Description: *A chicken-based cream soup with baked potatoes and onions.*

Ingredients

2 cups finely diced yellow onions
1/4 lb (1 stick) butter
1/2 cup flour
1 quart warm water
1/4 cup chicken bouillon
1 cup potato flakes
salt, pepper, garlic powder and

dried basil to taste
2 cups milk
2 cups heavy cream
1/2 teaspoon Tabasco
2 cups potatoes, diced but
    unpeeled

1. In large pot, saute onions in butter for 10 minutes or until tender; sprinkle flour over onions and continue to cook for 4 to 5 minutes longer, until flour is completely absorbed.
2. In bowl, combine water, chicken bouillon, potato flakes, and seasonings; whisk to combine; be sure mixture is lump-free. Pour mixture into onion mixture, 2 cups at a time.
3. Add milk, Tabasco and cream; continue whisking until smooth and slightly thickened. Reduce heat; simmer for 15 minutes, stirring occasionally.
4. Meanwhile, in separate pot, cover potatoes with water; bring to boil; simmer for 20 minutes or until potatoes are tender. Drain; add to creamed mixture and stir gently to combine. Serve hot.

Serves 4

About Houlihan's:

Houlihan's® first opened their doors in 1972, in Kansas City. At Houlihan's they make everything the hard way — from scratch. From appetizers and salads to entrees and desserts, it's all prepared fresh daily.

Howard Johnson's Boston Brown Bread

Description: *An old-fashioned molasses-sweetened brown bread that is sure to bring back many memories.*

Ingredients

1 cup unsifted whole-wheat flour
1 cup unsifted rye flour
1 cup yellow cornmeal
1 1/2 teaspoons baking soda

1 1/2 teaspoons salt
3/4 cup molasses
2 cups buttermilk
baked beans, to serve

1. Grease and flour 2-quart mold; set aside.
2. In bowl, combine flours, cornmeal, soda and salt; whisk to blend.
3. Stir in molasses and buttermilk; mix well; transfer to prepared mold and cover tightly with foil.
4. Insert a trivet in deep kettle and place mold on trivet. Pour boiling water along side of kettle (do not pour on mold) until it measures halfway up sides of mold; cover pan. Steam 3 ½ hours or until done.
5. Keep an eye on the water level so it does not boil down completely. Add boiling water as needed.
6. Remove from mold to cake rack. Serve hot with baked beans.

Makes 1 loaf.

About Howard Johnson's:

In 1925 Howard Deering Johnson took over his deceased father's failing businesses, one of which was a soda fountain and newsstand located in Wollaston, Massachusetts. Johnson developed a unique method of making ice cream by doubling the butterfat content and using only natural ingredients. The ice cream was such a hit with customers that it enabled Johnson to turn around the failing business and expand it into a chain of franchise restaurants catering to travelers.

In-N-Out Double-Double Hamburger

Description: Two all-beef patties, topped with classic American cheese, lettuce, tomato, onion and dressing served on a delicately toasted roll.

Ingredients

1 plain hamburger bun
1/3 lb. ground beef
dash salt
1 large lettuce leaf
sliced onions
2 slices American cheese

1 tablespoon Kraft Thousand
  Island dressing
1 large tomato slice (or 2 small
  slices)
1/2 tablespoon oil

1. Place skillet over medium heat; place split hamburger bun cut side down in pan and toast lightly; remove and set aside.
2. Meanwhile, form beef into two thin patties, slightly larger than the bun.
3. Place in skillet or on preheated grill; lightly salt and cook to desired doneness.
4. In saute pan, heat a bit of oil and add onion slices; fry until golden brown; remove from heat; set aside.
5. When patties are done, place 2 slices of cheese on each patty and allow to melt slightly.
6. Assemble burger: Heel of bun, dressing, tomato, lettuce, patty, fried onions, patty, crown of bun. Serve immediately.

Makes 1 hamburger.

About In-N-Out:

Harry Snyder opened the first drive-thru restaurant in Baldwin Park, California, in 1948. His menu was limited to hamburgers, fries, soft drinks and milkshakes. All beef was ground and formed into patties by the employees who also cut their fries by hand, broke lettuce leaves by hand, and made milkshakes from real ice cream.

Jack in the Box Eggnog Milkshake

Description: *Egg nog flavored milkshake - great for the holiday season.*

Ingredients

1 cup premium vanilla ice cream
1/3 cup premium eggnog
dash nutmeg (optional)

RecipeSecrets.net tip: Eggnog is usually found in your grocer's dairy section during the holiday season.

1. Place ingredients in blender and mix until well blended and smooth.
2. Pour into a tall serving glass and top with a dash of nutmeg, if desired.

Serves 1

About Jack in the Box:

Robert Peterson started the original Jack in the Box® in 1951 with a drive-thru restaurant in San Diego. Before 1980, Jack's mascot clown's existence was that as a fixture on the drive-thru speaker. The company decided an image change towards more "adult fare" was in order, and in a commercial, they blew up the drive-thru clown.

The Jack in the Box menu is extensive. There's not only the usual line of burgers but also an interesting line of alternates like egg rolls, bacon potato cheddar wedges, and tacos.

Jimmy Buffett's Margaritaville Restaurant Cheeseburger in Paradise

Description: *A fine burger made from beef chuck and seasoned just right. Served on a toasted bun, topped with cheese, lettuce, tomato, onions. Served with a pickle and fries.*

Ingredients

2 tablespoons kosher salt
1 tablespoon ground black pepper
1/2 tablespoon garlic salt
1/2 tablespoon onion salt
1 teaspoon celery salt
28 oz. fresh USDA choice beef chuck, diced
8 slices cheese of choice

4 sesame hamburger buns, toasted
8 leaves iceberg lettuce
4 slices tomato, 1/4-inch thick
4 slices red onion, 1/4-inch thick
4 toothpicks
4 pickle spears
2 lbs. Idaho potatoes, peeled, cut into fries and fried until golden brown

1. Prepare seasoning salt: In small bowl, combine kosher salt, pepper, garlic salt, onion salt and celery salt.
2. Preheat grill. Grind beef chunks using a meat grinder or food processor and shape into 4 patties, each weighing 7-oz..
3. Place burger on grill and season with seasoning salt. Turn halfway through cooking process and season second side. Grill to desired doneness. When just about done, place cheese on top to melt slightly.
4. Place burger on heel of bun and top with lettuce, tomato and onion. Top with crown of bun and secure with a wooden pick.
5. Serve immediately with fries alongside and a pickle spear.

Serves 4

About Jimmy Buffett's Margaritaville Restaurant:

Visiting a Margaritaville Cafe is an experience unlike any other... It's not just a dining destination, it's an entire change of latitude. Whether it's the Jumbies on stilts, the volcanos erupting with margaritas, the pool slide that wraps around the bar, or the frozen concoctions, a trip to Margaritaville will not soon be forgotten.

Joe's Crab Shack Buttered Parsley Potatoes

Description: *Parsleyed red potatoes that will compliment any entree.*

Ingredients

1 1/2 lbs. small red potatoes, cut into bite-sized chunks
1/4 teaspoon salt
2 tablespoons finely chopped parsley
4 tablespoons butter
salt and black pepper, to taste

1. Place potato chunks in medium saute pan; cover with water. Over medium heat, bring to a soft boil; cook, uncovered, until potatoes are fork-tender.
2. When potatoes are tender, drain completely and return to saute pan. Top with fresh parsley and butter; cover with lid and cook over low heat for 20 to 30 minutes, stirring gently several times to mix in parsley and butter.
3. When ready to serve, season with salt and pepper.
4. Serve hot.

Serves 4

About Joe's Crab Shack:

Specializing in crab dishes and delightful seafood, Joe's Crab Shack® is a fun place to be. The look of a shanty by the seaside helps create a casual environment that typically is popular with patrons and brimming with energy.

Joe's Crab Shack Harvest Bay Mahi Mahi

Description: *Grilled mahi mahi topped with garlic butter sauteed shrimp and mushrooms, tossed with Alfredo sauce.*

Ingredients

4 mahi mahi fillets
1/2 cup garlic butter
1/2 cup salad shrimp
1/2 cup sliced mushrooms
1 cup Alfredo sauce, store bought
1/2 teaspoon dill weed

RecipeSecrets.net tip: Any mild white fish can be substituted for mahi mahi.

1. Place mahi mahi on preheated grill; grill until cooked through and browned; remove from grill; set aside. Keep warm.
2. Meanwhile, in saute pan, melt garlic butter and add shrimp and mushrooms. Saute for 2 to 3 minutes.
3. Stir in Alfredo sauce; stir in dill weed. Heat through.
4. Place mahi mahi on serving dish and pour sauce over.
5. Serve hot.

Serves 4

Kenny Rogers Roasters BBQ Sauce

Description: A uniquely sweet BBQ sauce flavored with applesauce and easy to prepare.

Ingredients

1 cup applesauce
1/2 cup Heinz ketchup
1 1/4 cups light brown sugar, packed
6 tablespoons lemon juice
salt and pepper, to taste
1/2 teaspoon paprika
1/2 teaspoon garlic salt
1/2 teaspoon cinnamon

1. In heavy saucepan, combine all ingredients; mix well. Bring sauce to a boil; stir constantly for about 4 or 5 minutes.
2. Reduce heat to low; continue stirring for about another 5 minutes; make sure sugar has dissolved completely.
3. Allow to simmer without stirring for 15 minutes on the lowest possible heat setting; do not cover.
4. If using as a basting sauce for ribs or chicken while baking, keep warm by transferring to the top of a double boiler placed over simmering water.
5. Sauce may be cooled completely in refrigerator and stored in a covered container. Use within 30 days.

Makes about 2 cups.

About Kenny Rogers Roasters:

Kenny Rogers Roasters® opened in 1991 serving foods you would make at home — like roasted chicken with all your favorite sides to go with it.

KFC Cole Slaw

Description: *This semi-sweet slaw goes well with fried chicken, fish, or even sandwiches.*

Ingredients

6 1/2 tablespoons vegetable oil
3/4 cup chopped onions
1 cup sugar
4 1/2 teaspoons tarragon vinegar
2 1/2 cups Miracle Whip
2 carrots, finely chopped
2 heads cabbage, finely chopped

1. In bowl, combine oil, onions and sugar; add tarragon vinegar; fold in Miracle Whip.
2. In large bowl, combine carrots and cabbag; mix well.
3. Pour dressing over cabbage mix; stir well to combine.
4. Cover and refrigerate overnight.

Serves 8

KFC Gravy

Description: *A thick and creamy gravy for any of your favorite dishes.*

Ingredients

1 tablespoon vegetable oil
5 tablespoons all-purpose flour
1 can Campbell's chicken broth (plus 1 can of water)
1/4 teaspoon salt
1/8 teaspoon Accent Flavor Enhancer
1/8 teaspoon ground black pepper

1. In medium saucepan over low heat, combine oil with 1 ½ tablespoons flour. This is your roux. Heat mixture for 20 to 30 minutes, stirring often, until it is a dark chocolate color. Be careful not to burn - it will ruin the taste and you will have to start over.
2. Remove from heat; add remaining ingredients; mix well.
3. Increase heat to medium; place saucepan over heat. Bring gravy to boil; reduce heat; simmer 15 minutes, or until thick.

Makes about 3 cups.

KFC Potato Wedges

Description: *Seasoned potato wedges like the Colonel makes.*

Ingredients

shortening for frying
1 egg
1 cup milk
5 baking potatoes, cut into wedges
1 cup flour
2 tablespoons salt
1 teaspoon pepper
1/2 teaspoon Accent Flavor Enhancer

RecipeSecrets.net tip: If you can't find Accent, then add seasoned salt instead.

1. Preheat shortening to 375 degrees F.
2. In large bowl, combine egg and milk; mix well; set aside.
3. In separate bowl, combine dry ingredients and whisk well; set aside.
4. Cut potatoes into 16 to 18 wedges of equal size.
5. Place potato wedges in egg mixture; remove with slotted spoon and transfer to dry mixture; using fingers, turn and coat well. You may have to do this in batches.
6. Deep fry in hot oil for 5 minutes or until golden brown. Serve hot.

Serves 4-6

Lawry's Taco Seasoning

Description: *This recipe makes an equivalent of 1 envelope of taco seasoning.*

Ingredients

1 1/4 teaspoon chili powder
1 teaspoon paprika
1 teaspoon salt
3/4 teaspoon minced onion
1/2 teaspoon cumin
1/4 teaspoon cayenne pepper
1/4 teaspoon garlic powder
1/4 teaspoon sugar
1/8 teaspoon ground oregano

1 tablespoon flour

1. In small bowl, combine all ingredients. Store in an airtight container.

To prepare tacos:

1. Preheat a large skillet.
2. Brown 1 lb. ground beef; drain the fat.
3. Add Taco Seasoning and 2/3 cup water to the beef; mix thoroughly.
4. Bring to a boil, then reduce heat to low and cook, uncovered, about 10 minutes, stirring occasionally.
5. Serve taco filling with warmed taco shells or tortillas. Top with shredded lettuce, grated cheddar cheese and chopped tomato or fresh salsa.

Makes enough meat filling for 12 tacos.

Lipton's Onion Soup

Description: *Use this mix for making dips and dressings and also in your favorite recipes that call for an envelope of soup mix.*

Ingredients

3/4 cup minced onion
1/3 cup beef bouillon
4 teaspoons onion powder
1/4 teaspoon crushed celery seed
1/4 teaspoon sugar

1. Combine all ingredients.
2. Place in container with tight-fitting lid.

About 5 tablespoons of mix are equal to one 1.25-oz. package.

To make onion dip:

1. Mix 5 tablespoons onion soup mix with one pint of sour cream.

Lone Star Steakhouse Amarillo Cheese Fries and Dip

Description: *Baked fries smothered in cheese and bacon with a taco-flavored ranch dipping sauce.*

Ingredients

1 (8-oz.) bottle (1 cup) ranch salad dressing

1 (1.25-oz.) envelope taco seasoning

1 (32-oz.) package frozen spicy French fries, prepared as directed

4 strips crisply cooked bacon, crumbled

1/2 cup shredded Monterey Jack or Colby cheese

1. In small bowl, combine Ranch dressing and Taco seasoning; mix well and set aside.
2. Place cooked fries close together on baking sheet; sprinkle evenly with cheese and bacon; return to oven until cheese is melted.
3. Serve immediately with dipping sauce.

Serves 4

About Lone Star Steakhouse:

Lone Star restaurants feature an authentic roadhouse theme and serve mesquite-grilled steaks, which are hand-cut fresh daily at each restaurant. Their menu includes "Texas-sized" large portions of food, including a variety of combinations that are sure to please. Upbeat country and western music, Texas artifacts, and their excellent service standards enhance the Lone Star experience.

Lone Star Steakhouse Lone Star Chili

Description: *A delicious chili with a bit of a kick.*

Ingredients

1 lb. ground beef
1 diced onion
1 tablespoon diced fresh
jalapeno pepper
1 (15-oz.) can kidney beans
with liquid
1 (14.5-oz.) can peeled diced
tomatoes
1 (8-oz.) can tomato sauce
1 cup water
1 tablespoon white vinegar

1 teaspoon salt
1 teaspoon chili powder
1/4 teaspoon garlic powder
1 bay leaf

Garnish:
grated Cheddar cheese
diced onion
canned whole jalapeno chili
peppers

RecipeSecrets.net tip:
Alternatively, you can brown beef and saute onion and pepper; transfer to crockpot; cook on low 4 to 6 hours or on high 3 to 4 hours.

1. In large skillet, over medium heat, brown beef; drain.

2. Add onion and pepper; saute to soften, 4 to 5 minutes; add remaining ingredients.

3. Reduce heat and simmer for one hour, stirring occasionally.

4. To serve, ladle into bowls and top with cheese, onions and peppers.

Serves 4-6

Macaroni Grill Baked Creamy Seafood

Description: *Scallops, shrimp and clams covered in Asiago-fla-vored cream sauce and served with crispy wontons for dipping.*

Ingredients

4 tablespoons butter, divided
1 cup baby scallops, rinsed and drained (about 8 oz.)
3 tablespoons flour
2 cups half and half
1 1/2 cups Asiago cheese
2 cups medium, peeled, shelled and deveined cooked shrimp

1 (6-oz.) can chopped clams, well drained
1 to 2 tablespoons grated Parmesan cheese
oil for deep frying
1/2 of a 12-oz. package wonton skins

1. Over high heat, in large skillet, melt 1 tablespoon butter; add scallops and stir-fry until just cooked through; remove from skillet to bowl; set aside.

2. Using same skillet, melt remaining 3 tablespoons but-ter over medium heat; whisk in flour until smooth and bubbly; cook and stir for 1 minute.

3. Whisk in half and half; continue whisking until mix-ture comes to a boil; boil one minute, whisking, until bubbly. Turn off heat.

4. Whisk in Asiago cheese, whisking until melted. Stir in scallops, shrimp and clams.

5. Transfer seafood mixture to a 9-inch glass pie plate; sprinkle with Parmesan cheese and bake in preheated 350 degree F. oven for 15 minutes or until top is golden brown.

6. Meanwhile, heat about 1/2-inch oil in wok or deep fryer to 375 degrees F. Fry 3 or 4 wonton skins at a time, a few seconds on each side, just until golden; drain on paper towels.

7. Use wontons as chips for dipping in seafood.

Serves 4

About Romano's Macaroni Grill:

Romano's Macaroni Grill® bills itself as a chain of casual Italian dining restaurants located around the world. The first Romano's Macaroni Grill was opened in San Antonio, Texas, in 1988 by Phil Romano.

Macaroni Grill Chick l'Orange

Description: *Soy sauce-flavored chicken breast sliced with Andouille, carrots, peppers—seasoned with garlic and the flavor of citrus served over rice and steamed broccoli.*

Ingredients

8 to 10 oz. boneless, skinless chicken breast, sliced thin
2 oz. soy sauce
1/2 oz. olive oil
1/4 oz. diced carrots
1/4 oz. diced red bell pepper
1/4 oz. diced Andouille or smoked sausage
1/4 oz. diced celery

1/4 oz. diced onion
1 clove crushed garlic
1 splash white wine
1 cup orange juice
cooked white rice, to serve
steamed broccoli, to serve

RecipeSecrets.net tip:
If Andouille sausage is too spicy for you, substitute your favorite pork sausage.

1. With sharp knife, cut chicken breast in half, and then in half again from side to side.
2. Dip chicken pieces in soy sauce.
3. Place large skillet over medium-high heat; add oil and heat. Add carrots, red bell peppers and andouille; saute for 2 minutes; add celery and onion; saute another 2 minutes or until onions are clear and vegetables have a slight burning to the edges.
4. Add chicken, searing both sides, while scraping the bottom of the pan to prevent burning; add garlic.
5. Pour wine along edge of pan to de-glaze; add orange juice; reduce by half. You want a nice, rich brown sauce, with a slight hint of orange.

6. Serve with white rice and steamed broccoli.

Serves 4

Macaroni Grill Roasted Garlic Lemon Vinaigrette

Description: *The perfect combination of olive oil, red wine vinegar and garlic with a hint of citrus and sweetened with honey.*

Ingredients

1/4 cup red wine vinegar
3 tablespoons honey
1/2 teaspoon salt
1/2 oz. roasted garlic
3/4 cup virgin olive oil
1/2 lemon, juiced (no seeds)

1. Place vinegar, honey, salt and roasted garlic in bowl of food processor; puree until garlic is finely chopped.
2. With processor running, add olive oil and lemon juice.
3. Transfer to bowl; cover and refrigerate until ready to use.

Makes about 1 cup.

Mader's Black Forest Torte

Description: *An authentic German recipe - chocolate decadence topped with whipped cream, coating layers of cherries and more whipped cream.*

Ingredients

2 cups all-purpose flour
1/2 cup unsweetened cocoa powder
2 1/2 teaspoons baking powder
1/2 teaspoon salt
2 cups whole eggs (about 8 to 10 large)
2 cups granulated sugar
3/4 cup whole milk
3/4 cup solid vegetable shortening
vanilla extract, to taste

Kirschwasser, to taste (German cherry brandy)
1 (21-oz.) can cherry pie filling
3 half-pints whipped topping or sweetened whipped cream to measure at least 4 cups whipped
1 (17-oz.) can dark-sweet cherries, drained
chocolate shavings

1. Preheat oven to 325 degrees F. Grease two 9-inch round cake pans; set aside.

2. In large bowl, combine flour, cocoa powder, baking powder and salt; whisk to combine. Add eggs, sugar, milk, shortening and vanilla. With electric mixer, beat on high speed 10 minutes.

3. Divide batter equally between prepared cake pans; bake in preheated oven until cake springs back when touched.

4. Remove from pans to wire racks to cool completely. Using sharp serrated knife, slice each layer in half making 4 layers. Sprinkle each layer with some kirshwasser.

5. Place one layer on serving platter. Using a large pastry bag fitted with a large star tip, pipe a circle of whipped cream around circumference of cake layer;

place a circle of cherry filling inside the whipped cream. Continue alternating circles until layer is cov-ered.

6. Top with remaining cake layers, covering each in the same manner.

7. Using remaining whipped cream, frost entire cake.

8. Using same pastry bag, make 16 rosettes out of whipped cream. Place a cherry in the center of each rosette. Sprinkle top and sides with chocolate shav-ings.

9. Store in refrigerator.

Serves 12

About Mader's German Restaurant:

Mader's German Restaurant is located in Milwaukee, Wisconsin. Famous for their German cuisine, Mader's has had the pleasure of serving Presidents Kennedy, Ford, and Reagan. They've been in business for over 100 years and are well known for their fabulous foods.

Mader's Hungarian Goulash

Description: *The combination of beef sirloin and caramelized onions in a rich sauce; served with spaetzel and spinach.*

Ingredients

1/2 cup oil or 5 oz. lard
2 lbs. onions, sliced
1 1/2 teaspoons paprika
1 (2 lbs.) beef chuck, cut in
  2-inch cubes
1 pint beef stock
1 1/2 teaspoons tomato paste
1 teaspoon salt
1 teaspoon vinegar

rind of half a lemon, finely
  chopped
1 clove garlic, finely chopped
1 teaspoon caraway seed
water to thin goulash
potatoes or noodles, to serve

1. Heat oil in large, heavy pot; add onions and fry until golden brown, about 10 to 15 minutes; sprinkle with paprika; stir well. Add meat, cover and let meat brown lightly; stir frequently. Add stock; tomato paste, salt and vinegar.

2. Using a flat part of heavy knife or a mortar and pestle, mash lemon rind, garlic and caraway seeds; add to pot; stir.

3. Cover pot and simmer very gently for 30 minutes or until meat is tender, adding additional water in small quantities, if needed.

4. Serve with boiled potatoes, noodles or dumplings and a fresh, crusty roll.

Serves 4 - 5

McDonald's Apple Muffins

Description: *Apple pie filling—infused muffins conveniently made with a cake mix.*

Ingredients

21 oz. apple pie filling
3 eggs
2 teaspoons apple pie spice
18 oz. yellow cake mix

1. Preheat oven to 350 degrees F. Place paper liners in muffin tins; you will need two 12-cup tins; set aside.
2. In large bowl, combine all ingredients. With electric mixer, beat on medium speed to blend well.
3. Divide batter equally between muffin cups.
4. Bake in preheated oven for 25 to 30 minutes or until knife inserted in center comes out clean.
5. Remove to wire rack to cool completely.

Makes 2 dozen muffins.

About McDonald's:

In 1955, Ray Kloc opened in Des Plaines, Illinois - selling hamburgers for 15 cents. Since then McDonald's® has become the largest and fastes-growing fast-food chain in the world.

McDonald's Sweet & Sour Sauce

Description: *Peach and apricot preserves are the base for this easy and delicious dipping sauce.*

Ingredients

1/4 cup peach preserves
1/4 cup apricot preserves
2 tablespoons light corn syrup
5 teaspoons white vinegar
1 1/2 teaspoons cornstarch
1/2 teaspoon soy sauce
1/2 teaspoon yellow mustard
1/4 teaspoon salt
1/8 teaspoon garlic powder

2 tablespoons water

RecipeSecrets.net tip:
Pineapple preserves and orange marmalade also work as a substitution.

1. Place all ingredients (except water) in blender and puree until mixture is smooth.
2. Transfer to small saucepan and place over medium heat; add water; bring mixture to boil, stirring. Boil for 5 minutes, stirring often.
3. Remove from heat when sauce has thickened; cool completely.
4. Store in covered container in refrigerator.

Makes about 3/4 cup.

Mrs. Field's Black and White Cookies

Description: *Semisweet and white chocolate chunks of goodness make these drop cookies a family favorite.*

Ingredients

2 1/4 cups all-purpose flour
1/2 cup unsweetened cocoa
  powder
1/2 teaspoon baking soda
1/4 teaspoon salt
1 cup dark brown sugar; packed
3/4 cup white sugar
1 cup salted butter; softened

3 large eggs
2 teaspoons pure vanilla extract
5 1/4-oz. semisweet chocolate
  bar - chopped coarsely
5 1/4-oz. white chocolate bar,
  chopped coarsely

1. Preheat oven to 300 degrees F.
2. In medium bowl, combine flour, cocoa, baking soda and salt; whisk to combine; set aside.
3. In large bowl, combine sugars and butter; cream well using medium speed of electric mixer, scraping down sides of bowl.
4. Add eggs and vanilla; continue to beat until smooth.
5. Gradually add dry ingredients, mixing on low speed until just combined; do not over mix. Stir in chocolates.
6. Drop rounded tablespoonfuls of dough onto ungreased baking sheets, placing 2 inches apart to allow for spreading.
7. Bake in preheated oven for 20 to 25 minutes or until done.
8. Remove to wire racks to cool completely.

Makes 3 dozen cookies.

About Mrs. Fields:

The first Mrs. Fields store, in Palo Alto, California, opened August of 1977. Mrs. Fields has nearly 390 locations in the U.S., and over 80 locations internationally.

Old Spaghetti Factory Original Clam Sauce

Description: *A creamy, seasoned clam sauce served over noodles.*

Ingredients

3 oz. butter
2 garlic cloves, finely chopped
1/2 medium onion, finely chopped
3 medium celery ribs (outside peeled), finely chopped
3 tablespoons flour

2 cans (6-oz.) chopped clams
1 quart half and half
1/4 teaspoon ground thyme
1 teaspoon salt
hot cooked noodles (for serving)

1. In saucepan, over medium-low heat, combine butter, garlic, onion and celery; braise until tender but do not brown.
2. Add flour; mix well to make a roux. The mixture will thicken.
3. Drain clams; reserve juice.
4. In a separate saucepan, combine reserved clam juice, half and half, thyme and salt; heat to just below boiling; add to roux; cook until sauce thickens.
5. Add clams to sauce; stir gently to mix well.
6. Serve over cooked noodles.

Serves 6

About Old Spaghetti Factory:

Opening in 1969, in Portland, Oregon, Old Spaghetti Factory customers dine amidst old world antiques collected from around the world, while savoring perfectly cooked pasta and spaghetti sauces, freshly made using only the finest ingredients.

Olive Garden's Bistecca di Manzo alla Boscaiola

Description: *Rib eye steaks smothered in a tomato, onion, garlic, mushroom white wine sauce.*

Ingredients

1 oz porcini mushrooms, dried
1/2 cup white wine dry
2 cups canned diced tomatoes, with juice
2 tablespoons chopped fresh oregano
salt, to taste

black pepper, to taste
1/3 cup olive oil
4 ea. 1/2 " thick rib eye steaks
2 cloves garlic, finely chopped
1 yellow onion, sliced
chopped fresh parsley, for garnish

1. In small bowl, place dried porcini mushrooms and add warm water to cover; allow to soak for 20 minutes. Drain and coarsely chop. Transfer to saute pan.

2. Add white wine, tomatoes with juice and oregano; bring sauce to boil over medium heat; season to taste with salt and pepper. Reduce heat; simmer for 15 minutes.

3. In large skillet, heat oil over medium heat. Place steaks in hot oil and fry 4 minutes per side; add garlic and onions; cook an additional 2 minutes.

4. Transfer onions to serving platter; place steaks on top of onions. Pour mushroom sauce over steaks. Garnish with chopped parsley. Serve immediately.

Serves 4

Olive Garden Brownie Banana Funtastico

Description: *A delicious chocolate brownie covered with pineapple, surrounded by banana and then topped with banana mousse followed by whipped cream, chocolate topping, nuts and a cherry.*

Ingredients

1 package brownie mix
pineapple topping
bananas, as needed
whipped cream
chopped walnuts
chocolate topping
maraschino cherries

Banana Mousse:
1 envelope whipped topping mix
1/2 cup milk
1 package banana instant
  pudding mix (can use
  chocolate or strawberry)
1 cup milk

1. Prepare brownie mix according to package directions. Cool; cut.
2. In medium bowl, prepare whipped topping; beat topping with ½ cup milk for 5 minutes; transfer to clean bowl; set aside.
3. Using same bowl, add pudding mix and 1 cup milk; using electric mixer, beat on low for 2 minutes. Fold whipped topping into pudding mixture until well mixed. Cover and refrigerate.
4. To assemble: Place a brownie in a large bowl and spread with pineapple topping. Cut a banana in half lengthwise and place along sides of brownie in bowl. Top brownie with banana mousse and top with whipped cream; sprinkle with nuts, drizzle with chocolate topping and finish off with a cherry.

Serves 4-6

Olive Garden Chicken Castellina

Description: *Sauteed chicken smothered in a delicious cream sauce with pancetta, sun-dried tomatoes and fresh cheeses and served over your favorite pasta.*

Ingredients

Sauce:
1/4 cup diced pancetta
  (or bacon)
6 tablespoons butter, cubed
1 teaspoon garlic, chopped
1/4 cup diced sun-dried
  tomatoes
1 1/2 cups heavy cream
1 1/2 cups milk
1 oz cornstarch
1/4 cup grated Parmesan cheese
1/2 cup chopped smoked Gouda
  cheese
1/4 teaspoon salt
1 tablespoon chopped fresh
  rosemary
1 (8.5-oz.) can sliced artichokes,
  drained
1/4 teaspoon pepper

1/4 cup sliced mushrooms
1 1/2 lbs pasta of choice,
  cooked according to package
  directions

Chicken:
3/4 cup flour
1/2 teaspoon salt
1/4 teaspoon pepper
1 1/2 lbs skinless/boneless
  chicken breasts, cut in 1 - 1 ½"
  pieces
3 tablespoons olive oil
1/4 cup white wine

chopped fresh parsley,
  for garnish

1. Prepare sauce: Place pancetta (or bacon, if desired) in 3-quart saucepan. Turn heat on medium-high and cook until crisp and golden; reduce heat; add butter and melt; add garlic and sun-dried tomatoes. Saute mixture for about a minute, stirring frequently; do not brown.

2. Whisk in cream, milk and cornstarch; increase heat to medium-high; whisk in Parmesan and Gouda. Once the cheese has melted and is whisked smooth, add remaining sauce ingredients; bring to boil, stirring constantly.

3. Remove from heat and let stand; do not cover.

4. Prepare chicken: In shallow dish, combine flour, salt and pepper; whisk to combine. Dredge chicken in mixture, coat well and shake off excess flour.

5. In large heavy skillet, heat olive oil; add chicken in a single layer; cook until golden brown on both sides and juices run clear.

6. CAUTION WITH THIS STEP: Add wine to pan (you will get a low flame in the pan from the alcohol). Toss gently until wine has evaporated. Add reserved cheese sauce; bring to boil over medium-high heat; heat through.

7. Meanwhile, cook pasta al dente (to the bite); drain; do not rinse. Transfer to large serving platter. Top with chicken and pour sauce over. Serve hot.

Serves 4

Olive Garden Chicken con Zucchini

Description: *Rigatoni covered with sauteed zucchini slices and smothered in a tomato - mushroom sauce infused with the fine blend of Italian seasonings.*

Ingredients

Sauce:
1/3 cup olive oil
1 cup chopped onion
1 lb. fresh mushrooms, divided
1 1/2 teaspoons minced garlic
3 cups crushed tomatoes
16 oz. canned tomatoes, diced and drained
1 1/2 cups tomato puree
1 cup black olives, sliced and drained
2 teaspoons capers, drained
1/2 teaspoon dried oregano
1/2 teaspoon dried basil

1/4 teaspoon black pepper
1/4 teaspoon crushed red pepper
1/2 teaspoon fennel seeds
1/2 teaspoon salt

Zucchini:
4 large zucchini, sliced lengthwise 1/4-inch thick
2 tablespoons olive oil
dried basil
dried oregano
salt and black pepper
1 lb. rigatoni, cooked
grated Parmesan cheese

1. Prepare sauce: Cut half the mushrooms into quarters; set aside. Finely mince remaining mushrooms.

2. In large heavy skillet over medium heat, heat olive oil; add onion and finely minced mushrooms. Saute 10 minutes, stirring frequently, until onions are soft.

3. Add garlic and quartered mushrooms; cook for 5 minutes, stirring constantly. Do not let this mixture stick or burn. Add remaining sauce ingredients; bring to simmer, reduce heat and simmer for 20 minutes, stirring frequently.

4. Meanwhile, slice zucchini and sprinkle with salt, pepper, basil and oregano.

5. In large skillet, heat 1 tablespoon olive oil over medium heat and place zucchini slices in skillet in single layer, sautéing about 3 minutes per side until tender. Do this in batches, removing cooked zucchini to platter and covering to keep warm until all the zucchini is cooked. Add more olive oil as needed.

6. Place pasta on serving platter. Ladle sauce generously over pasta; top with cooked zucchini slices; sprinkle with Parmesan cheese. Serve hot.

Serves 4

Olive Garden Chicken Milanese

Description: *Cheese and Italian seasoning-flavored chicken breasts in a white wine and chicken-based cream sauce infused with tomatoes and spinach served over tortellini.*

Ingredients

Sauce & Pasta:
1/2 cup unsalted butter
4 garlic cloves, minced
1/4 cup all-purpose flour
1 cup white wine
1 cup chicken broth
1 cup heavy cream
1 cup grated Parmesan cheese
8 roasted garlic cloves, minced
 (or 4 tablespoons)
1/4 teaspoon black pepper, to
 taste
1/2 teaspoon salt
8 cherry tomatoes, halved
1/4 cup chopped spinach
1 (20-oz) package tortelloni or
 tortellini, cooked according to
 package directions

Chicken:
4 tablespoons extra-virgin olive
 oil
4 boneless, skinless chicken
 breasts
3 large eggs
1/4 cup milk
1 cup Panko breadcrumbs
1/2 cup grated Parmesan cheese
3 teaspoons fresh parsley,
 chopped
1 1/2 teaspoons Italian
 seasoning
1 tablespoon chopped garlic
1/4 teaspoon black pepper
1/2 cup flour
4 lemon wedges

1. Prepare chicken: Place chicken between 2 sheets of plastic wrap; pound gently to ½-inch thickness.
2. In shallow dish, whisk eggs and milk until blended.
3. In small bowl, combine breadcrumbs, cheese, parsley, Italian seasoning, garlic and pepper; transfer to separate shallow dish.
4. Dredge chicken in flour; press to coat both sides; dip in egg wash to coat both sides; allow excess to shake off. Place in breadcrumbs, pressing to coat well on both sides. Set aside. Allow to sit on a plate to set.

5. Prepare sauce: In saucepan, over medium heat, melt butter; add minced garlic; saute for 1 minute; add 1/4 cup flour; stir until well blended. Add wine, broth, heavy cream and cheese. Bring to boil; reduce heat and simmer, allowing mixture to thicken. When mixture begins to thicken, add roasted garlic, pepper and salt; stir to blend well. Add tomatoes and spinach; allow to simmer over low heat for 5 minutes, stirring frequently.

6. Cook chicken: In large, heavy skillet heat olive oil over medium-high heat. Add chicken to pan and cook until both sides are golden brown and internal temperature reaches 165 degrees F.

7. Meanwhile, cook tortellini in boiling salted water; drain and do not rinse.

8. Transfer tortellini to serving platter and top with cooked chicken and sauce. Garnish with fresh parsley and lemon wedges. Serve hot.

Serves 4

Olive Garden Chicken Scampi

Description: *Chicken breasts sauteed with bell peppers, roasted garlic and onions in a garlic cream sauce over angel hair pasta.*

Ingredients

olive oil
2 chicken breasts, sliced
bell peppers, thinly sliced
red onions, thinly sliced
10 cloves of garlic, roasted
1/2 package angel hair pasta,
  cooked and drained

White Sauce:
1 tablespoon butter
2 tablespoons flour
3/4 cup hot milk

Scampi Sauce:
3 tablespoons butter
2 tablespoons crushed garlic
3/4 teaspoon crushed red
  pepper flakes
2 tablespoons Italian seasoning
black pepper, to taste
3/4 cup white wine
1 cup chicken broth
1/4 cup white sauce

1. Prepare the white sauce: Heat 1 tablespoon butter in a sauce pan, add 2 tablespoons flour and cook for 2 minutes on medium heat, stirring constantly. Slowly add hot milk (hot so it won't get lumpy). Set aside. Keep warm.

2. Prepare the scampi sauce. In sauce pan, heat butter over low heat; add the garlic, Italian seasoning, crushed red pepper, Italian seasoning and black pepper. Cook for about 2 minutes on low heat. Add the wine and chicken broth. Stir until combined and simmer about 30 minutes. Add the white sauce and cook until slightly thickened.

3. In a large skillet, saute chicken in a little olive oil until almost done. Add the peppers and onions, then saute until chicken is cooked through. Add the scampi sauce. Saute until everything is warmed. Add roasted garlic cloves. Serve over pasta. Pour a little of the leftover white sauce over the dish.

Serves 2

Olive Garden Chocolate Chip Cookie Dough Cheesecake

Description: The fabulous combination of chocolate chip cookie dough and chocolate chips in a creamy cheesecake filling atop a chocolate cookie crust.

Ingredients

2 tablespoons margarine
2 1/2 cups chocolate cookie crumbs
2 lbs. cream cheese, softened
1 cup granulated sugar
4 eggs
1 teaspoon all-purpose flour
1 teaspoon vanilla extract
1 cup sour cream

1 lb. refrigerated chocolate chip cookie dough
2 oz. chocolate chips

Toppings:
1 pint heavy whipping cream, whipped
chocolate chips
chopped walnuts

1. Preheat oven to 325 degrees F.
2. Generously grease the bottom and sides of a 10-inch springform pan.
3. Combine the margarine with the chocolate cookie crumbs. Press onto the bottom and sides of the pan. Set aside.
4. Using an electric mixer on high speed, combine cream cheese, sugar, eggs, and flour and mix until smooth.
5. Add vanilla extract and sour cream and mix just until blended. Pour 1/2 of the batter into prepared crust.
6. Cut cookie dough into golf ball-size chunks and drop into batter. Sprinkle in chocolate chips. Pour into crust. Bake for 60 minutes.
7. Turn off the oven and open the oven door (to the broil position on some ovens). Allow cake to remain in the oven 30 more minutes. Let cool. Refrigerate until serving.
8. To serve, remove the sides of the pan and top with fresh whipped cream. Sprinkle with additional chocolate chips and chopped walnuts. This cheesecake is best refrigerated overnight before serving.

Serves 8

Olive Garden Eggplant Parmigiana

Description: *Lightly breaded eggplant, fried and covered with tomato-meat sauce, and topped with mozzarella cheese.*

Ingredients

1 large eggplant, peeled, and cut into 1/4-inch-thick slices
flour, for dusting
seasoned salt, to taste
oil, for frying
1 (16-oz.) jar meat-flavored sauce
1/4 cup grape jelly
1 (14-oz.) can sliced-style stewed tomatoes
8 slices mozzarella cheese

1. Preheat oven to 375 degrees F. Lightly oil or spray jelly roll pan, set aside.

2. Slice eggplant (you should have 8 slices) and moisten slices; coat lightly in flour and season lightly with salt. Using large heavy skillet, heat oil and brown eggplant; transfer to jelly roll pan. Cover loosely with foil and bake in preheated oven until tender, about 20 minutes.

3. Prepare sauce: Place saucepan over medium heat and add sauce, jelly and tomatoes (break tomatoes with a fork). Heat through, do not boil. Stir to melt jelly completely.

4. To serve: Place 2 slices of eggplant on each oven-proof plate; cover each eggplant slice with a slice of mozzarella cheese; drizzle sauce over without covering completely; place plate in oven to melt cheese. Serve immediately.

Serves 4

Olive Garden Gameroni al'Aglio

Description: *Sauteed shrimp, onion and garlic in a butter-wine sauce over angel hair pasta.*

Ingredients

2 tablespoons olive oil
1 medium onion
3 garlic cloves (crushed)
1 1/2 lbs. medium fresh
  shrimp, shelled
4 oz. butter
1/2 cup white wine
crushed red pepper, to taste

salt, to taste
pepper, to taste
10 oz. angel hair pasta
3 tablespoons finely chopped
  parsley

RecipeSecrets.net tip: Substitute chicken broth for the wine if desired.

1. In saute pan, heat oil; add onion; saute 2 minutes. Add garlic and saute additional minute.
2. Add shrimp; cook 1 to 2 minutes.
3. Add butter and wine. Season to taste with red pepper, salt and pepper.
4. Meanwhile, cook pasta in boiling salted water until al dente (to the bite); drain; do not rinse.
5. Transfer drained pasta to serving platter and top with shrimp mixture; sprinkle with parsley. Serve hot.

Serves 4

Olive Garden Gnocchi with Spicy Tomato and Wine Sauce

Description: *Fresh potato dumplings smothered in a spicy tomato and wine sauce and topped with Parmesan and fresh basil.*

Ingredients

2 tablespoons extra-virgin olive oil
6 cloves fresh garlic
1/2 teaspoon chili flakes
1 cup dry white drinking wine
1 cup chicken broth
2 (14 1/2-oz.) cans tomatoes
1/4 cup (1/2 stick) sweet cream butter, cut into 1-inch cubes, chilled

1/2 cup freshly grated Parmesan cheese
salt, to taste
freshly crushed black pepper, to taste
1 lb. gnocchi (potato dumplings)
freshly chopped basil, to taste

1. Prepare sauce: Do not preheat skillet; place olive oil, garlic and chili flakes in pan. Place pan over medium heat; stir until garlic is slightly browned; add wine and broth; simmer for 10 minutes.

2. Reduce wine/broth mixture by half; add tomatoes; continue to simmer for 30 minutes more.

3. Transfer to blender; add butter and Parmesan cheese; season to taste with salt and pepper; puree.

4. Meanwhile, cook pasta in boiling salted water until they float, about 3 minutes; drain; transfer to serving platter.

5. Pour sauce over; toss lightly to coat. Garnish with Parmesan and basil. Serve hot.

Serves 4

Olive Garden Grilled Shrimp Caprese

Description: *Marinated shrimp atop angel hair pasta, topped with melted mozzarella and tomatoes in a garlic-butter sauce.*

Ingredients

Marinated Tomatoes:
1 1/2 lbs Roma tomatoes, cored and cut into 1" pieces
20 medium fresh basil leaves, stems removed and cut into 1" pieces
2 tablespoons extra-virgin olive oil
1 tablespoons minced garlic
1 teaspoon Italian seasoning
salt, to taste

2 tablespoons butter
1/2 cup white wine
1 1/2 cups heavy cream
1 cup grated Parmesan cheese
1 lb capellini (angel hair) pasta, cooked according to package directions
2 cups shredded mozzarella cheese
1 lb 26/30 or 21/25 shrimp, peeled and deveined

RecipeSecrets.net tip:
To preserve juices and seeds, use a pairing knife to remove just the top of the core on each tomato.

1. In large bowl, combine tomatoes, basil, olive oil, garlic, Italian seasoning and salt; mix well. Cover; set aside and allow to marinate for at least 1 hour.

2. Preheat broiler.

3. Place a large, non-stick skillet over medium heat, melt butter in hot skillet; stir in wine; bring to boil; add heavy cream and Parmesan cheese; bring to simmer and allow to reduce to desired consistency. Do not let mixture boil once the cream has been added to the pan.

4. Meanwhile, cook pasta in boiling salted water; drain; do not rinse. Add to sauce; add marinated tomatoes; mix well, coating pasta.

5. Transfer to ovenproof serving platter, top with mozzarella cheese; place in broiler to melt cheese.

6. Meanwhile, cook shrimp by grilling or saute in pan; internal temperature should read 150 degrees F when done. Place shrimp over melted cheese and serve hot.

Serves 4-6

Olive Garden Pasta with Broccoli

Description: *Pasta smothered in broccoli-studded Béchamel sauce.*

Ingredients

12 oz broccoli florets; steamed
1/4 cup olive oil
2 teaspoons minced garlic
1/4 cup thinly sliced green
 onions
1 cup sliced fresh mushrooms
2 teaspoons chopped fresh
 parsley
1 lb fresh pasta shells

Parmesan; grated

Béchamel Sauce:
1/4 cup butter or margarine
1/4 cup flour
1 quart milk
2 teaspoons chicken bouillon
 granules or 2 cubes, mashed

1. Prepare Béchamel sauce: In 2-quart saucepan, melt butter over medium heat; stir in flour; cook 1 minute. Add milk and bouillon; whisk vigorously until mixture barely comes to a boil. Do not boil milk. Reduce heat and allow to simmer 5 minutes, whisking vigorously frequently. Keep warm.

2. Divide prepared broccoli in half; chop one half into ¼-inch pieces; set aside.

3. Heat a large saute pan over medium heat; add olive oil and heat; add all the broccoli, garlic, green onions and mushrooms; cook; stir constantly for 2 minutes or until mushrooms begin to turn golden.

4. Add broccoli mixture and parsley to warm sauce; stir well to blend.

5. Meanwhile, cook pasta in boiling salted water until al dente (to the bite); drain; do not rinse; transfer to serving platter. Pour sauce over and top with Parmesan. Serve hot.

Serves 4

Outback Steakhouse Aussie Fries

Description: *French fries sprinkled with shredded Colby-jack cheese and crisp bacon; served with a kicked-up sour cream dipping sauce.*

Ingredients

oil for frying
1 lb. bag of frozen french
fries
1 cup shredded Colby Jack
cheese
6 strips of bacon, cooked

Dipping Sauce:
1/2 cup sour cream
1 tablespoon horseradish
dash cayenne pepper
dash salt and pepper

1. Prepare dipping sauce: Combine all sauce ingredients; blend well. Cover and refrigerate until ready to serve.
2. Heat oil to 350 degrees F in a large, heavy skillet.
3. Fry the potatoes in small batches, until golden brown.
4. Drain the fries on paper towels. Keep them warm in a 250 degree F oven until all the fries are done.
5. Place the cooked fries onto a plate. Salt the fries to taste, and sprinkle with cheese and cooked bacon.
6. Place back into a warm oven until the cheese begins to melt.
7. Serve with dipping sauce.

Serves 4-6

About Outback Steakhouse:

Outback® was founded in Florida in 1987. At the time, the 1986 movie Crocodile Dundee had become a big hit. The Outback was kind of the wild, wild west of Australia. So they brought the Australian western theme to the restaurant.

Outback Steakhouse Sydney's Sinful Sundae

Description: *Scoops of vanilla ice cream over a bed of toasted coconut and covered with a warm chocolate sauce, whipped cream and a fresh strawberry.*

Ingredients

1 cup shredded coconut
4 large scoops vanilla ice cream
1/2 cup Hershey chocolate syrup
whipped cream (in a can)
4 large, ripe strawberries

1. Preheat the oven to 300 degrees F.
2. Spread the coconut over the bottom of a large oven pan. Shake the pan a little to spread the coconut evenly.
3. Bake the coconut for 25 to 30 minutes or until the coconut is a light, golden brown. You may have to stir or shake the coconut in the last 10 minutes to help it brown evenly.
4. When the coconut has cooled, pour it onto a plate or into a large bowl. Roll each scoop of ice cream in the coconut until it is well coated. Press down on the ice cream to help the coconut stick. Place the ice cream into 4 separate bowls.
5. Heat the chocolate syrup for 10-15 seconds in the microwave. Pour about 2 tablespoons over each scoop of ice cream. Try to completely cover the ice cream with chocolate.

6. Spray some whipped cream on the top of each scoop of ice cream.

7. Cut the stems from the strawberries and place one on each serving upside down on the whipped cream. Serve with a spoon.

Serves 4

RecipeSecrets.net tip:
Substitute chopped nuts for the coconut in this recipe.

P. F. Chang's China Bistro Dan Dan Noodles

Description: *Ground chicken and egg noodles in a chicken-based sauce. Garnished with bean sprouts and cucumbers.*

Ingredients

Noodles:
1 teaspoon oil
1/2 teaspoon chili paste
1/2 teaspoon garlic, minced
1/4 oz. green onion, minced
4 oz. ground chicken, cooked
1/4 oz. egg noodles, cooked
cornstarch

Liquid Mixture:
2 oz. soy sauce
1 oz. cooking wine
1 teaspoon oyster sauce
1 teaspoon granulated sugar
7 oz. chicken stock

Garnish:
bean sprouts
julienned cucumber

1. Using large skillet or wok, heat the oil; add chili paste, garlic and green onion; sear for 5 seconds. Do not inhale the direct fumes.
2. Add cooked ground chicken, toss and stir for 10 to 15 seconds; add all liquid ingredients; simmer for 20 seconds.
3. Make a slurry of cornstarch and water (1 to 2 teaspoons of each) and add to wok. This will thicken your sauce. The sauce should be thick enough to stick to the top of the noodles.
4. Pour sauce over a plate of hot cooked noodles and garnish with bean sprouts and julienned cucumbers.

Serves 4

About P. F. Chang's China Bistro:

P. F. Chang's® is unique. It blends classic Chinese design with a modern bistro look. Each location features an original handpainted mural depicting scenes of life in 12th century China. The goal of a P. F. Chang's meal is to attain harmony of taste, texture, color and aroma.

P.F. Chang's China Bistro Orange Peel Chicken

Description: *Lightly coated pieces of chicken with a hint of citrus served with a tangy tomato-based sauce.*

Ingredients

Sauce:
1 tablespoon vegetable oil
2 tablespoons minced garlic
4 green onions, sliced
1 cup tomato sauce
1/4 cup granulated sugar
2 tablespoons chili garlic sauce
1 tablespoon soy sauce

Chicken:
1/2 cup vegetable oil
4 boneless, skinless chicken
  breasts
1 egg, beaten
1 cup milk
1 cup flour
peel from 1/4 orange, julienned
  (into 1/8"-thick strips)
cooked white or brown rice,
  to serve

1. Prepare the sauce: In medium saucepan, heat oil; add garlic and onions; do not let the garlic burn; add tomato sauce; bring to boil.

2. Add sugar, chili sauce and soy sauce; bring to boil; simmer 5 to 6 minutes or until sauce thickens; remove from heat.

3. Prepare chicken: In wok or large skillet, heat oil. Meanwhile cut chicken breasts into bite-sized pieces.

4. In medium bowl combine egg and milk; mix well. Place flour in shallow dish.

5. Coat chicken pieces - first in the flour, then the egg wash and back into the flour. Cook in 2 or 3 batches until all chicken is cooked.

6. When chicken is done, remove oil and rinse out wok with water; reheat pan. When hot, add orange peel and chicken; heat through - about a minute - stirring gently. Add sauce; heat through.

7. Serve with white or brown rice.

Serves 4

P.F. Chang's China Bistro Singapore Noodles

Description: *Rice sticks combined with stir-fried chicken, shrimp and vegetables.*

Ingredients

2 gallons water
1 lb. rice sticks (available at Asian markets)
4 tablespoons canola oil, divided use
8 oz. medium-size shrimp
8 oz. chicken, julienned
1 tablespoon garlic, chopped
1 cup julienned cabbage
1/2 cup julienned carrots
2 medium tomatoes, diced large

1 cup Singapore Sauce (page 117)
1 bunch scallions (green parts only), cut 2 inches long
1/4 bunch cilantro, roughly chopped
1 teaspoon sesame oil
1/3 cup fried shallots (optional, available at Asian markets)
1 lime, quartered, for garnish

1. Bring water to a rolling boil. Place rice sticks into boiling water for 2 minutes (just until soft), then drain into a colander.
2. Immediately rinse under rapid-running hot water for 1 minute. Drain well (the noodles still should be slightly warm). Toss with 2 tablespoons of the oil; set aside.
3. In a hot wok, stir-fry shrimp and chicken with remaining 2 tablespoons oil just until done, approximately 2 minutes.
4. Add garlic, cabbage, carrots and tomatoes and stir-fry for 1 minute. Add rice sticks and stir-fry for 1 minute. Add Singapore Sauce; stir-fry until all ingredients are well incorporated, approximately 2 minutes. Add scallions, cilantro and sesame oil; toss briefly.
5. If desired, sprinkle fried shallots all over the noodles; garnish with a lime wedge.

Serves 4

P.F. Chang's China Bistro Singapore Sauce

Description: *A spicy sauce to use with your favorite Chinese and Oriental dishes.*

Ingredients

2 tablespoons white vinegar
1/4 cup Madras curry powder
pinch turmeric (optional)
1/4 cup light soy sauce
1 cup vegetarian oyster sauce
1/4 cup Sriracha chile sauce
1/4 cup ketchup

1. Combine vinegar, curry powder and turmeric (if using).
2. Mix well until powders are well dissolved.
3. Add soy, oyster and chile sauces and ketchup; mix well.

Makes about 2 cups.

P.F. Chang's China Bistro Spicy Chicken

Description: *Wok-seared chicken in a tasty sauce with just a bit of a kick.*

Ingredients

1 cup vegetable oil
2 chicken breast fillets
1/3 cup cornstarch
rice, to serve

Sauce:
2 teaspoons vegetable oil
2 tablespoons chopped garlic (3 to 4 cloves)
3 tablespoons chopped green

onions (about 3 onions)
1 cup pineapple juice
2 tablespoons chili sauce
2 tablespoons white distilled vinegar
4 teaspoons sugar
1 teaspoon soy sauce
2 tablespoons water
1/2 teaspoon cornstarch

1. Prepare sauce: Heat 2 teaspoons vegetable oil in medium saucepan; add garlic and onion; saute just a bit — do not let burn.
2. Immediately add pineapple juice, chili sauce, vinegar, sugar and soy sauce. In small bowl, dissolve cornstarch in water; add to pan.
3. Bring mixture to a boil; simmer over medium-high heat for 3 to 5 minutes or until thick with a syrupy consistency.
4. In wok or large skillet, heat 1 cup oil over medium heat. Meanwhile, chop chicken into bite-sized pieces. Toss chicken in cornstarch, dusting well. Add chicken to oil; saute until light brown. Drain on paper towels.
5. Transfer to serving bowl, add sauce and toss to coat. Serve immediately with rice on the side.

Serves 2

Pizzeria Uno's Chicago Deep Dish Pizza

Description: *A classic deep dish pizza with a wonderful thick crust topped with a fine selection of sausage, cheese and tomatoes.*

Ingredients

Pan Dough:
1 cup warm tap water (110-115 degrees F)
1 package active dry yeast
3 1/2 cups flour, divided use
1/2 cup coarse ground cornmeal
1 teaspoon salt
1/4 cup vegetable oil

Pizza Topping:
1 lb Italian sausage, removed from the casing and crumbled
1 can whole tomatoes, drained and coarsely crushed
1 lb mozzarella, sliced thin
2 cloves garlic, peeled and minced
5 fresh basil leaves, chopped fine
4 tablespoons freshly grated Parmesan cheese

1. Combine warm water and yeast; stir to blend and allow to sit for 5 minutes - until it foams. Add 1 cup of flour, all of the cornmeal, salt, and vegetable oil. Mix well with a spoon. Continue stirring in the rest of the flour 1/2 cup at a time, until the dough comes away from the sides of the bowl. Flour your hands and the work surface and knead the ball of dough until it is no longer sticky.

2. Let the dough rise in an oiled bowl, sealed with plastic wrap, for 45 to 60 minutes in a warm place, until it is doubled in bulk. Punch it down and knead it briefly. Press it into an oiled 15-inch deep dish pizza pan, until it comes 2 inches up the sides and is even on the bottom of the pan. Let the dough rise 15 to 20 minutes before filling.

3. Preheat the oven to 500 degrees F.

4. While the dough is rising, prepare the topping. Cook the crumbled sausage until it is no longer pink; drain off excess fat. Chop tomatoes and strain.

5. When the dough has finished its second rising, lay the mozzarella over the dough shell. Then distribute the sausage and garlic over the cheese.

6. Top with the tomatoes. Sprinkle with the seasonings and Parmesan cheese.

7. Bake in preheated 500 degree F oven for 15 minutes; reduce oven temperature to 400 degrees F and bake for 25 to 35 minutes longer. Lift up a section of the crust from time to time with a spatula to check on its color. The crust will be golden brown when done. Serve immediately.

RecipeSecrets.net tip: Make your own blend of grated Italian cheeses for added flavor. Use any combination of Asiago, mozzarella, provolone, fontina, etc.

Serves 8

About Pizzeria Uno:

Pizzeria Uno started as a Chicago-style pizza place in Chicago selling pasta and sandwiches as well. It was opened in 1943 by Ike Sewell.

Red Lobster Alaska Snow Crab with Red Sauce

Description: *Steamed crab legs served with a tomato-based sauce.*

Ingredients

1 1/2 lbs. Alaska snow crab clusters, single-cut legs
2 tablespoons minced onion
1 garlic clove, minced
1 tablespoon butter or margarine
1 (8-oz.) can tomato sauce
1/4 cup ketchup
1/4 teaspoon crushed oregano

1. Rinse crab under cool running water and cut into serving-size pieces. Using a heavy knife score the backs of leg sections or slit using kitchen shears.
2. In saute pan or wok, saute onion and garlic in butter. When tender, stir in remaining ingredients except crab. Simmer 5 minutes.
3. Serve hot with chilled or steamed crab.

Serves 4

Red Lobster Fried Soft Shell Crab

Description: Soft shell crabs in a lightly seasoned coating, sautéed and baked until crispy.

Ingredients

18 live soft shell crabs
1 teaspoon salt
1/4 teaspoon ground black
  pepper
1/4 teaspoon garlic powder
1/4 teaspoon onion powder
2 oz. lemon juice

3 dashes soy sauce
1 cup all-purpose flour
3 eggs, beaten with
  3 tablespoons water
2 cups plain bread crumbs
oil, for frying
cocktail sauce, for serving

1. Clean crabs; do not remove top shell; using cool water - rinse well.

2. Place on large sheet pan. Combine salt, pepper, garlic powder and onion powder, lemon, soy sauce; season crabs; cover and refrigerate at least 2 hours.

3. When ready to cook, place flour in shallow dish; beat eggs in another shallow dish and place breadcrumbs in another shallow dish. Coat crabs in flour, shake off excess; dip in egg wash; shake off excess; dredge in bread crumb coating well. Place on plate till ready to cook.

4. Preheat oven to 450 degrees F. Meanwhile, heat about an inch of oil in heavy skillet. Place crabs in hot oil cooking on one side for 4 to 5 minutes; turn and continue to cook until browned and crispy.

5. Transfer to baking sheet and place in preheated oven for 8 minutes to heat all the way through.

6. Serve with sauce of choice: cocktail sauce, Dijon sauce or a Remoulade sauce.

RecipeSecrets.net tip:
Top the crab with some fresh lemon wedges and melted butter. Serve with cocktail sauce.

Serves 4

Red Lobster Hawaiian Skewers

Description: *Shrimp, scallop, pineapple and bell pepper kebobs basted with a barbecue and salsa sauce.*

Ingredients

1/2 lb. shrimp, peeled and deveined
1/2 lb. bay or sea scallops
1 can pineapple chunks, drained (reserve juice)
1 green bell pepper, cut in wedges
bacon slices

Sauce:
6 oz. barbecue sauce
16 oz. salsa
2 tablespoons pineapple juice
2 tablespoons white wine

1. In bowl, combine sauce ingredients and blend well.
2. If using bamboo skewers, soak in water for 30 minutes. Preheat grill.
3. When ready to serve, skewer pineapple chunks, shrimp, scallops, bell pepper wedges, and bacon slices (folded in half).
4. Baste evenly on each side with sauce; place on pre-heated grill.
5. Cook until shrimp are pink in color. Do not overcook or shrimp will be rubbery.
6. Serve hot with white rice.

Serves 4

Red Lobster Shrimp Scampi

Description: *Baked shrimp in a butter-wine sauce.*

Ingredients

1/2 cup unsalted butter
1 cup white wine
3 tablespoons minced garlic
1 lb. shrimp, peeled and deveined
salt and pepper, to taste

1. Preheat oven to 350 degrees F.
2. Place butter, wine, garlic and shrimp in ovenproof skillet; place in preheated oven and bake until shrimp turn pink, about 7 minutes. Do not overcook or shrimp will be rubbery.
3. Season to taste with salt and pepper. Serve hot.

Serves 2-4

Red Robin Banzai Burger

Description: *Teriyaki marinated beef burgers grilled to desired doneness served on a toasted roll with a grilled pineapple slice, Cheddar cheese, lettuce, tomato and mayonnaise.*

Ingredients

teriyaki sauce
ground beef for patties

For each patty you will need:
2 slices canned pineapple
1 sesame seed hamburger bun
2 slices Cheddar cheese
shredded lettuce
2 tomato slices
mayonnaise

1. Form ground beef into patty; marinate in teriyaki sauce, turning to flavor both sides.
2. When ready to cook, remove from marinade and discard marinade. Place patty on preheated grill. Cook to desired doneness.
3. Grill sliced pineapple on both sides.
4. Toast bun; this prevents serving a mushy burger.
5. Assemble sandwich: Place patty on heel of bun, top with grilled pineapple, cheddar cheese, lettuce, tomato and mayo; top with crown of bun. Serve immediately.

RecipeSecrets.net tip:
A combination of ground beef and pork goes very well with this recipe.

Makes 1 burger.

About Red Robin:

Red Robin® first opened their doors in Seattle, Washington in 1969. Their focus is on serving an imaginative selection of high-quality gourmet burgers in a family-friendly atmosphere.

Red Robin Five Alarm Burger

Description: *Crank up the heat with Pepper-Jack cheese, jalapeños, fresh tangy salsa, sliced tomato, crisp lettuce and Chipotle mayo.*

Ingredients

Chipotle Mayonnaise:
1/4 cup mayonnaise
1/4 teaspoon ground chipotle
  chile pepper
1/8 teaspoon paprika

1- 5.5-oz. ground beef patty
1/4 teaspoon (approximately)
  Red Robin Seasoning salt
  (see page 127)

2 slices Pepper Jack cheese
1 sesame seed hamburger bun
4 to 6 jalapeno slices
2 tablespoons fresh salsa or pico
  de gallo
1/3 cup shredded iceberg
  lettuce

1. Prepare chipotle mayonnaise: In small bowl, combine all ingredients; mix well. Cover and refrigerate until ready to serve. Will store well for a week in the refrigerator.

2. Preheat grill.

3. Prepare patty: Shape beef into a patty that is slightly larger than the bun; season with seasoning; place on grill, seasoned side down and season top side. Grill to desired doneness. Just before burger is done, place pepper jack cheese on top and allow to melt a bit.

4. Meanwhile, toast bun and spread with chipotle mayonnaise. Place patty on heel of bun; top with jalapeno slices and salsa or pico de gallo. Place shredded lettuce over salsa and place crown of bun on top. Serve immediately.

Serves 1

Red Robin Seasoning-Salt

Description: *This seasoning salt is a definite staple for all pantries. Use on any of your burgers, steaks, chicken, etc.*

Ingredients

3 tablespoons salt
1 tablespoon instant tomato soup mix
2 teaspoons chili powder
¼ teaspoon cumin
¼ teaspoon black pepper

1. Combine all ingredients.
2. Store in an airtight container.

Makes 1/3 cup,

RecipeSecrets.net tip:
Keep a jar of this in your pantry to use on other meat dishes.

Ritz Carlton Baked Chocolate Mousse

Description: All the pleasures of a warm flourless chocolate souffle cake baked in this fabulously smooth dessert.

Ingredients

butter and sugar for coating
  ramekins
5 egg whites
1 teaspoon sugar
pinch of salt

9 oz dark chocolate
4 egg yolks
whipped cream, for garnish
chocolate sprinkles, for garnish

1. Preheat oven to 340 degrees F. Generously butter oven-proof ramekins; sprinkle with sugar, shaking to coat; pour out excess sugar; set aside.
2. In medium bowl, beat egg whites, sugar and salt until stiff.
3. Melt chocolate in top of double-boiler; stir in egg yolks.
4. Carefully fold half of beaten egg whites into chocolate; mix gently; add remaining egg whites; mix gently.
5. Pour mixture into prepared ramekins. Place filled ramekins in a deep baking pan; carefully fill with water halfway up sides of ramekins without splashing water in filled ramekins. Bake 25 to 30 minutes.
6. Carefully remove ramekins from hot water to dish towel to dry sides of ramekins. Discard hot water.
7. Invert onto individual plates or on a platter. Garnish with a dollop of whipped cream and chocolate sprinkles.

Serves 7

About Ritz Carlton:

Cesar Ritz created a luxurious hotel setting. Offering exquisite service, the staff dressed in proper uniforms, from white tie and apron uniforms for the wait staff, black tie for the Maitre d' and morning suits for all other staff, creating a formal, professional atmosphere. He had à la carte dining, which provided gourmet cuisine choices for diners.

Ro Tel's Famous Cheese Dip

Description: *A zesty kick of smooth cheese with diced tomatoes and green chilies makes this a perfect party cheese dip.*

Ingredients

1 lb. pasteurized process cheese spread, cubed (such as Velveeta)
1 can (10 oz.) Ro Tel diced tomatoes and green chilies, original,
  milder, or extra hot
tortilla chips, crackers or vegetables, for serving

1. In a medium saucepan, combine cheese spread and Ro Tel tomatoes. Heat over low heat until cheese is melted, stirring frequently.
2. Serve with tortilla chips, crackers or vegetables.

Makes about 2 cups of dip.

Microwave Directions:

1. Place ingredients into a covered, microwave-safe bowl. Microwave on HIGH, about 5 minutes or until cheese is melted. Stir once during heating.

About Ro-Tel:

Carl Roettele opened a small family canning plant in Elsa, Texas, during the 1940s. His theory was simple; fresh ingredients and unique blends of products would deliver a flavorful addition to recipes in his home state of Texas. He used the freshest, most flavorful tomatoes, adding chopped green chili peppers and a special blend of spices to create a sensational taste.

Ruby Tuesday Sonoran Cheese Sauce

Description: *A thick cheese sauce with the addition of salsa and sour cream.*

Ingredients

6 tablespoons butter
1/2 cup finely chopped onion
1 small clove garlic, minced
1/3 cup all-purpose flour
1 cup hot water
1 tablespoon chicken stock
1 cup half and half
salt to taste
1/2 teaspoon sugar
1/4 teaspoon hot pepper sauce,
  or more to taste

1 teaspoon lemon juice
1/4 teaspoon cayenne pepper
3/4 cup shredded Parmesan
  cheese
3/4 cup cubed Velveeta cheese
3/4 cup prepared salsa (medium
  hot)
1/2 cup sour cream

1. In medium saucepan, melt butter; add onion and garlic; saute until onion is transparent and not browned. Whisk in flour to make a roux; continue to whisk, cooking for 5 minutes.

2. In large glass measuring cup, combine hot water, chicken stock, and half and half; pour slowly into saucepan, whisking constantly; cook for an additional 5 minutes. Your sauce should have the consistency of honey.

3. Add salt, sugar, hot sauce, lemon juice, cayenne and Parmesan cheese; whisk to blend well. Do not let mixture boil.

4. Add Velveeta cubes and continue to whisk; add salsa and sour cream; blend well.

Makes 5 cups.

About Ruby Tuesday:

This restaurant was formed in 1972, when Sandy Beall and four of his fraternity buddies from the University of Tennessee opened the first restaurant adjacent to the college campus in Knoxville. Today Ruby Tuesday® is one of three large public companies that dominate the bar-and-grill category of casual dining.

Saks Fifth Avenue Tomato-Basil Bisque

Description: *A creamy enhancement of the traditional tomato soup — sure to please.*

Ingredients

3 tablespoons butter
1 large yellow onion
1/2 rib celery
3 tablespoons flour
1 tablespoon minced garlic
2 cans (16-oz.) diced tomatoes
2 tablespoons chopped fresh
   basil

2 cans (16-oz. size) tomato
   puree
1 can (16-oz. size) beef stock
1/2 cup heavy whipping cream
1 bay leaf
salt and pepper, to taste

1. In large stockpot, melt butter; add diced onion and celery; saute until onion is transparent and not browned.
2. Sprinkle flour over mixture, one tablespoon at a time, stirring thoroughly after each addition, to form a paste.
3. Add garlic, diced tomatoes and basil; blend well. Stir in puree; slowly add beef stock, then whipping cream. The soup will have a rose color.
4. Add bay leaf; simmer over low heat for about an hour. Remove bay leaf before serving. Adjust seasoning with salt and pepper.

Serves 8

About Saks Fifth Avenue:

Horace Saks and Bernard Gimbel opened Saks Fifth Avenue in 1924 — a unique specialty store of fashionable items. Today it is the savvy shopper's premier source for designer clothing and accessories.

Sbarro Baked Ziti

Description: Ziti cut pasta, with creamy ricotta, melted mozzarella and Romano cheeses and seasoned tomato sauce.

Ingredients

2 lbs. ziti (uncooked)
2 lbs. ricotta cheese
3 oz. grated Romano cheese
3 cups garlic & onion tomato sauce, store bought
1/2 teaspoon black pepper
1 1/2 lbs. shredded mozzarella cheese

1. In large pot of boiling salted water, cook ziti 12 to 14 minutes until al dente to the bite, stirring often. When done, drain and do not rinse.
2. Meanwhile, preheat oven to 350 degrees F.
3. In large bowl, combine ricotta, Romano, 2 3/4 cups tomato sauce and pepper; blend well. Add cooked ziti; mix well.
4. Transfer remaining tomato sauce to 13 X 9 X 2-inch baking pan; spread over bottom of pan.
5. Transfer ziti to baking pan; top with mozzarella cheese. Cover loosely with foil. Bake in preheated oven until cheese is melted and ziti is heated through, about 15 to 20 minutes.
6. Serve hot with garlic bread and additional sauce, if desired.

Serves 6-8

Sbarro Tomato Sauce

Description: *A classic tomato sauce, perfectly seasoned for any of your pasta dishes.*

Ingredients

1-2 oz. olive oil
10 oz. diced onions
1 oz. chopped fresh garlic
3 oz. Sherry cooking wine
1/2 oz. chopped fresh Italian
  parsley
2 - (28-oz.) cans crushed
  tomatoes
1 - tomato can cold water
4 oz. grated Romano cheese

Spices:
2 tablespoons salt
2 teaspoons dried oregano
1/2 teaspoon crushed red
  pepper flakes
1/2 teaspoon black pepper
2 teaspoons dried basil

1. In large skillet, heat oil until hot — do not allow to smoke. Add onions; saute until almost browned; add garlic and brown lightly.
2. De-glaze pan with sherry; add parsley; blend well.
3. Add tomatoes, water, cheese and spices; blend well.
4. Bring just to boil; reduce heat; simmer for 1 hour.

Shoney's Country Fried Steak

Description: *Lightly breaded and seasoned cube steaks deep fried and served with a chicken-based cream sauce.*

Ingredients

2 cups flour
2 teaspoons salt
1/4 teaspoon black pepper
3 cups water
4 (4 oz.) cube steaks,
  trimmed, flattened

Gravy:
1 1/2 tablespoons ground beef,
  lean
1/4 cup flour
1/4 teaspoon salt
1/4 teaspoon black pepper
2 cups chicken broth
2 cups milk

1. In bowl, sift flour, salt and pepper together; set aside.
2. In separate bowl, pour water. Dip steaks in water, shaking off excess.
3. Press steaks into flour mixture to coat well; shake off excess; place on waxed-paper-lined baking sheet and place in freezer for 3 hours.
4. When ready to cook, preheat oil in deep fryer to 350 degrees F.
5. Meanwhile, make gravy: Brown beef in skillet; stir in flour; blend well. Add remaining gravy ingredients; bring to boil, reduce heat and simmer until thick.
6. At the same time, cook steaks in hot oil for 8 to 10 minutes; drain on paper towels.
7. To serve, pour hot gravy over steaks.

Serves 4

Shoney's Slow-Cooked Pot Roast

Description: *The old-fashioned goodness of the perfect comfort food. Slow-cooking makes the meat just melt in your mouth.*

Ingredients

2 tablespoons butter
3 lbs rump roast, trimmed
2 celery ribs, chopped
1 large onion, chopped
3 garlic cloves, minced
1/2 teaspoon dried parsley
1/2 tablespoon dried thyme
2 cups beef broth
20 whole peppercorns

1 whole bay leaf
1/2 tablespoon salt
2 carrots, sliced
2 potatoes, peeled and cubed
1/2 teaspoon salt
1/3 cup flour

1. Preheat oven to 325 degrees F.
2. Melt butter in Dutch oven; add roast and brown on all sides; remove to platter. Add celery, onion, garlic, parsley and thyme to Dutch oven; saute 5 minutes; return roast to Dutch oven.
3. Add broth, peppercorns, bay leaf and salt; cover; place in preheated oven. Cook roast 4 hours; baste every 30 minutes.
4. When done, remove roast and strain stock into bowl; discard vegetables. Using two forks, shred meat into bite-sized pieces and return to Dutch oven. Pour strained broth over shredded beef; add carrots, potatoes and salt. Return to oven and cook for 45 additional minutes.
5. Drain and measure stock from Dutch oven. Add enough beef broth to measure 3 cups and place in saucepan. Whisk in flour; simmer until thick. Pour over meat and vegetables.

Serves 6

Sonic Drive-In Ocean Water

Description: *Beware of the blue tongue side effect from this delicious drink.*

Ingredients

3 tablespoons water
2 tablespoons sugar
1 teaspoon coconut extract
2 drops blue food coloring
2 12-oz. cans cold Sprite
ice, to fill 2 glasses

RecipeSecrets.net tip: You can substitute diet soda.

1. In small bowl, combine water and sugar; microwave for 30 to 45 seconds, stir to dissolve all the sugar; allow to cool.

2. When cool, add coconut extract and food coloring; stir well to blend.

3. Stir in 2 cans cold Sprite into syrup; blend well. Divide and pour over ice. Add straws and serve.

Makes two 12-oz. servings.

About Sonic Drive-In:

The first Sonic® was opened in Oklahoma, originally called the Top Hat. It now has several locations across America. Carhops with roller skates deliver the orders to your car.

Subway's Crusty Honey 'n Oats Bread

Description: *A bread machine recipe for making a healthy and delicious bread.*

Ingredients

2 packets of active dry yeast
1/2 cup old-fashioned oatmeal
1 cup buttermilk
1 large egg
1 1/2 cups sifted all-purpose
  flour
1 1/2 cups whole-wheat flour
2 tablespoons honey
1 1/2 teaspoons salt

melted butter
Italian herb mixture
dried Monterey Jack cheese
grated Parmesan cheese
toasted oats

RecipeSecrets.net tip:
An Italian herb mixture includes basil, oregano, thyme, marjoram, rosemary, savory, and sage.

1. Combine yeast, buttermilk, egg, flours, oatmeal, honey and salt in bread machine pan.
2. Turn bread machine on light setting; cook according to manufacturer's directions.
3. When done, remove to wire rack to cool.
4. Brush cooled bread with melted butter; sprinkle lightly with Italian herbs, dried jack cheese, grated Parmesan, and toasted oats.

About Subway:

Subway® is the world's largest submarine sandwich chain with more than 30,000 restaurants in 87 countries.

Taco Bell Crispitos

Description: *Deep-fried tortilla chips sprinkled with cinnamon and sugar - serve with honey.*

Ingredients

1/8 cup cinnamon
1/2 cup sugar
10 flour tortillas

oil for deep frying
honey, to serve

1. In small bowl, combine cinnamon and sugar; mix well.
2. In large skillet or Dutch oven, heat oil to 350 degrees F.
3. Cut tortillas in quarters; deep fry a few at a time for 30 seconds or until golden brown on both sides. Remove to paper towels to drain.
4. Immediately sprinkle with cinnamon/sugar mixture.
5. Serve with honey for an added treat.

Serves 6-8

Texas Roadhouse Ranch Dressing

Description: *A creamy dressing for your favorite salads. Can be used on sandwiches or as a dipping sauce.*

Ingredients

3/4 cup mayonnaise
1/4 cup buttermilk
1/2 teaspoon garlic powder
1/4 teaspoon cayenne
1/4 teaspoon freshly cracked black pepper
dash dried, minced garlic

RecipeSecrets.net tip:
Make your own buttermilk. For this recipe combine 1/4 cup milk and 2 teaspoons lemon juice or white vinegar. Let stand for 10 minutes before using.

1. Combine all ingredients, blending well. Store in covered container in refrigerator.

Makes about 1 cup.

About Texas Roadhouse:

Texas Roadhouse got its start in Clarksville, Indiana in 1993. Their main focus is on steaks and ribs. They cut their steaks on site and make everything the old-fashioned way — homemade.

T.G.I. Friday's French Onion Soup

Description: *A delicious French onion soup topped with Italian cheese over sliced French baguette.*

Ingredients

3-4 medium to large onions
butter
3 cans of beef broth
2 bay leaves
dash of garlic powder
salt and pepper, to taste
Worcestershire sauce
3/4 cup water
French baguette

8 oz. bag Italian cheese blend

1. Slice the onions into rings and saute in butter in a skillet until tender.

2. Meanwhile, pour beef broth in crockpot and turn on LOW. Add bay leaves, garlic powder, salt and pepper; add 2 tablespoons Worcestershire sauce and ¾ cup water. When the onions mixture is tender, add to crockpot.

3. Cover and cook for at least 3-5 hours on low. At this point you may want to taste the soup and see if you would like it a little weaker-if so add a little water or chicken broth. Also, at this time remove the bay leaves and discard them.

4. When ready to serve, slice bread into thin slices and toast in oven on 350 or in toaster oven until just crusty. Ladle hot broth over bread and cover with cheese, adjusting cheese to your liking. The cheese will melt and the bread will float to the top. Serve hot.

Serves 4-6

About T.G.I. Friday's:

T.G.I. Friday's®, one of the first American casual dining chains, is a dining experience that has become
the favorite pastime of millions since 1965. The first
T.G.I. Friday's was located at First Avenue and 63rd
Street in New York City. Their focus is on providing a
comfortable, relaxing environment where guests can
enjoy quality food and have a good time.

T.G.I. Friday's Lemon Chicken Scaloppini

Description: *Chicken and mushrooms with a hint of citrus in a cream-based Chablis sauce over pasta and artichokes.*

Ingredients

Chicken:
2 1/2 lbs. chicken breast (pounded thin)
2 oz. olive oil
8 oz. sliced mushrooms
2 lemons (halved)
4 oz. heavy whipping cream
4 artichokes, halved
4 teaspoons parsley
12 oz. lemon sauce
20 oz. angel hair pasta

8 tablespoons fried pancetta
4 tablespoons fried capers

Lemon Sauce:
1 quart Chablis
1 tablespoon fresh lemon juice
3 teaspoons butter
1 quart whipping cream
1 tablespoon thyme
1 teaspoon salt
1 teaspoon pepper

1. Prepare sauce: Boil Chablis to reduce to 2 cups. Add lemon juice and butter; melt slowly. Add whipping cream and simmer over low heat until thickened. Add spices and cool to room temperature.

2. Chicken: Heat saute pan over medium heat. Add oil and heat. Add chicken pieces and saute on each side for one minute (or until no longer pink).

3. Add sliced mushrooms and saute with chicken for an additional minute. When mushrooms are cooked, squeeze juice from lemons into saute pan and coat the chicken with juice (ensure there are no seeds).

4. Add cream to pan and stir to incorporate. Bring to a boil. Cut artichoke halves in half again lengthwise, add to pan and cook for 15 seconds.

5. Remove pan from heat. Add parsley and stir to incorporate. Add lemon sauce and stir to incorporate. Do not return pan to heat.

6. In large bowl, twirl pasta into a nest. Sprinkle chick-
en pieces over pasta and pour remaining contents of
pan on and around the chicken. Sprinkle pancetta
and capers over the entire dish. Garnish with
chopped parsley.

Serves 4

RecipeSecrets.net tip:
Use bacon in place of
pancetta.

T.G.I. Friday's Mandarin Orange Sesame Dressing

Description: A honey-sweetened citrus-flavored sesame dressing to serve over salad greens with chicken on top.

Ingredients

1/3 cup orange marmalade
1/2 teaspoon cayenne pepper
1/4 teaspoon ground ginger
1/4 teaspoon garlic powder
1/4 cup white vinegar
2/3 cup vegetable oil
2 tablespoons soy sauce
3 tablespoons sesame oil
2 tablespoons honey

1/4 cup mandarin orange
  sections, chopped

Salad:
mixed greens
grilled chicken breasts

1. Place marmalade, cayenne pepper, ginger, garlic powder, vinegar, oil, soy sauce, sesame oil and honey into blender container. Cover and blend on medium speed 30 to 45 seconds. Transfer to small bowl; stir in chopped orange sections, blending well. Cover and refrigerate. This will last for 3 days in refrigerator.

If making a salad:

1. Drizzle over a bed of mixed greens, topped with sliced, grilled chicken breasts.

Serves 4

T.G.I. Friday's Spicy Cajun Chicken Pasta

Description: *A tangy sauce bathes juicy chicken and ribbons of fettuccine.*

Ingredients

10 oz. cooked fettuccine
(cooked al dente)
1 cup Spicy Cajun Pasta Sauce
(recipe follows)
1 boneless chicken breast,
cooked and sliced in strips
1 tablespoon Parmesan cheese
1 teaspoon chopped parsley

Spicy Cajun Pasta Sauce:
2 oz. olive oil
1 tablespoon fresh chopped
garlic
1/2 cup coarsely chopped onion

1/2 cup coarsely chopped green
peppers
1/2 cup coarsely chopped red
peppers
1/8 teaspoon cayenne pepper
1 cup chicken stock
1 cup V-8 juice
cornstarch (mix about a table
spoon with a couple
tablespoons cold water to form
a slurry)
salt and pepper, to taste

1. Prepare sauce: Heat oil in saute pan; add garlic; saute for 30 seconds; add onions and saute for 1 minute; add peppers and continue to saute for another minute. Deglaze with chicken stock and reduce to half. Add V-8 juice and cayenne pepper; bring to boil; simmer 10 minutes.

2. Thicken to consistency with cornstarch; season to taste with salt and pepper.

3. Add cooked pasta to sauce and heat through until hot.

4. Arrange on serving dish and top with chicken breast. Sprinkle with Parmesan and parsley.

Serves 4

Tony Roma's Chocolate Martini

Description: *A smooth cocktail with a tasty blend of chocolate and creme liqueur.*

Ingredients

2 oz. vanilla vodka
2 oz. Amaretto
2 oz. Baileys Irish Cream
2 oz. Kahlua
2 oz. chocolate syrup

1. Mix together and chill.

Serves 1

RecipeSecrets.net tip:
Serve in a martini glass.
Garnish with fresh berries
or chocolate shavings.

Trader Joe's Heroic Baklava

Description: *A rich, sweet pastry made of layers of phyllo dough filled with chopped nuts and sweetened with honey.*

Ingredients

1 lb. phyllo dough
1/2 lb. butter, melted

Nut Filling:
1 1/2 lbs. walnuts, unsalted
  toasted/ coarsely chopped
1 cup sugar
1 1/2 teaspoons ground
  cinnamon
1/2 teaspoon ground cloves

Syrup:
1 cup honey
3/4 cup water
1/4 cup sugar
2 tablespoons lemon juice
1 small piece lemon peel
1 small piece orange peel
1 1-inch cinnamon stick

1. Preheat oven to 350 degrees F. Butter 13 X 9 X 2-inch baking pan; set aside.

2. Prepare filling: In small bowl, combine nuts, sugar, ground cinnamon and cloves; mix well and set aside.

3. Prepare syrup: In heavy saucepan, combine honey, water, sugar, lemon juice, lemon and orange peels, and cinnamon stick. Bring to simmer and simmer for 10 minutes. Cool. When cool, remove peels and discard. Set aside.

4. Thaw phyllo dough; unwrap and fold entire amount in half, like the pages of a book. Keep a damp towel to cover as you are working. Turn over one sheet at a time and using a soft brush, brush with melted butter; repeating until 1/3 have been brushed with butter.

5. Lay flat in bottom of prepared baking pan. Spread ½ of nut filling over top.

6. Brush another 1/3 of sheets; place over nuts in pan, laying flat. Top with remaining nut mixture.
7. Brush remaining sheets and lay on top. Brush top sheet with remaining butter.
8. Using a sharp knife, score pastry into diamonds without cutting through to bottom. Make diagonals by cutting horizontal cuts across pan, then across diagonally from one end of each horizontal line.
9. Place in preheated oven and bake for 35 to 40 minutes or until puffed, crisp and deep golden in color.
10. Remove from oven and pour cooled syrup over baklava.
11. Let stand 4 hours. When cool, cut through to bottom layer in scored cuts.

Makes about 24 pieces.

About Trader Joes:

Started in the 1950s as a small chain of convenience stores and evolved into selling innovative, hard-to-find, great-tasting foods under the "Trader Joe's" name. Now they have over 300 stores and continue to grow.

V8 Juice

Description: *A healthy, so-good-for-you drink to enjoy straight up or to cook with. An excellent source of vegetable nutrition.*

Ingredients

8 carrots, cut into chunks
4 ribs of celery, cut into chunks
6 tomatoes, cut into chunks
1 bunch of fresh spinach
handful of parsley
1/2 medium white onion
1 fresh beet, cut into chunks
2 cloves fresh garlic

1. Place all ingredients in blender or juicer. Blend on high until thoroughly combined.
2. Stir, chill and serve.

Serves 2

RecipeSecrets.net tip:
This recipe can be used in a wide variety of recipes that call for vegetable juice or tomato juice.

Waldorf-Astoria Hotel Waldorf Salad

Description: *The traditional apple, walnut and chopped celery salad served on a bed of greens is updated with a yogurt and mayonnaise citrus dressing.*

Ingredients

1 cup walnut halves
1/2 cup mayonnaise
1/4 cup plain yogurt
1 teaspoon prepared mustard
pinch of dry mustard
juice of 1/2 lemon
4 to 6 tart apples, peeled,
   cored, and diced (2 cups)
1 to 2 cups finely diced inner
   ribs celery (white part only),
   leaves reserved

salt and freshly ground black
   pepper
2 bunches tender greens, such
   as arugula, baby kale,
   or pepper cress, washed and
   dried
2 tablespoons olive oil
1 tablespoon fresh lemon juice

1. Preheat the oven to 325°F.
2. Spread the walnuts on a baking sheet and toast in the oven for 4 to 5 minutes, until aromatic and lightly toasted. Let cool.
3. In large bowl, combine the mayonnaise, yogurt, both mustards, and the lemon juice. Fold in the apples and diced celery. Season with salt and pepper.
4. In large bowl, place the salad greens. Add the olive oil and lemon juice, season with salt and pepper, and toss well. Divide the greens among 4 plates. Spoon the apple mixture onto the greens and sprinkle with the toasted walnuts and garnish with reserved celery leaves.

Serves 4

About Waldorf-Astoria Hotel:

This famous luxury hotel in New York City first started as two different hotels: one owned by William
Waldorf Astor, whose 13-story Waldorf Hotel was
opened in 1893, and the other owned by his cousin,
John Jacob Astor IV, called the Astoria Hotel and
opened four years later and four stories higher.
Once combined it became the largest hotel in the
world at that time.

HELPFUL COOKING TIPS

1. Always chill juices or sodas before adding to beverage recipes.

2. Store ground coffee in the refrigerator or freezer to keep it fresh.

3. Seeds and nuts, both shelled and unshelled, keep best and longest when stored in the freezer. Unshelled nuts crack more easily when frozen. Nuts and seeds can be used directly from the freezer.

4. To prevent cheese from sticking to a grater, spray the grater with cooking spray before beginning.

5. Fresh lemon juice will remove onion scent from hands.

6. Instant potatoes are a good stew thickener.

7. Three large ribs of celery, chopped and added to about two cups of beans (navy, brown, pinto, etc.), will make them easier to digest.

8. When cooking vegetables that grow above ground, the rule of thumb is to boil them without a cover.

9. A scoop of sugar added to water when cooking greens helps vegetables retain their fresh color.

10. Never soak vegetables after slicing; they will lose much of their nutritional value.

11. To cut down on odors when cooking cabbage, cauliflower, etc., add a little vinegar to the cooking water.

12. Perk up soggy lettuce by soaking it in a mixture of lemon juice and cold water.

13. Egg shells can be easily removed from hard-boiled eggs if they are quickly rinsed in cold water after they are boiled.

14. Keep bean sprouts and jicama fresh and crisp up to five days by submerging them in a container of water, then refrigerating them.

15. When trying to reduce your fat intake, buy the leanest cuts you can find. Fat will show up as an opaque white coating or can also run through the meat fibers, as marbling. Stay away from well-marbled

cuts of meat.

16. Pound meat lightly with a mallet or rolling pin, pierce with a fork, sprinkle lightly with meat tenderizer, and add marinade. Refrigerate for about 20 minutes, and you'll have tender meat.

17. Marinating is easy if you use a plastic bag. The meat stays in the marinade and it's easy to turn and rearrange.

18. It's easier to thinly slice meat if it's partially frozen.

19. Tomatoes added to roasts will help to naturally tenderize them.

20. Cut meats across the grain; they will be easier to eat and have a better appearance.

21. When frying meat, sprinkle paprika over it to turn it golden brown.

22. Always thaw all meats in the refrigerator for maximum safety.

23. Refrigerate poultry promptly after purchasing. Keep it in the coldest section of your refrigerator for up to two days. Freeze poultry for longer storage. Never leave poultry at room temperature for more than two hours.

24. If you're microwaving skinned chicken, cover the baking dish with vented clear plastic wrap to keep the chicken moist.

25. Lemon juice rubbed on fish before cooking will enhance the flavor and help maintain a good color.

26. Scaling a fish is easier if vinegar is rubbed on the scales first.

27. Over-ripe bananas can be peeled and frozen in a plastic container until it's time to bake bread or cake.

28. When baking bread, a small dish of water in the oven will help keep the crust from getting too hard or brown.

29. Use shortening to grease pans, as margarine and oil absorb more readily into the dough or batter (especially bread).

30. To make self-rising flour, mix 4 cups flour, 2 teaspoons salt, and 2 tablespoons baking powder, and

store in a tightly covered container.

31. Hot water kills yeast. One way to tell the correct temperature is to pour the water over your forearm. If you cannot feel either hot or cold, the temperature is just right.

32. When in doubt, always sift flour before measuring.

33. When baking in a glass pan, reduce the oven temperature by 25 degrees.

34. When baking bread, you get a finer texture if you use milk. Water makes a coarser bread.

35. To make bread crumbs, toast the heels of bread and chop in a blender or food processor.

36. Cracked eggs should not be used as they may contain bacteria.

37. The freshness of eggs can be tested by placing them in a large bowl of cold water; if they float, do not use them.

38. Dust a bread pan or work surface with flour by filling an empty glass salt shaker with flour.

39. To slice meat into thin strips for stir-fry dishes, partially freeze it so it will be easier to slice.

40. To keep cauliflower white while cooking, add a little milk to the water.

41. A roast with the bone in will cook faster than a boneless roast. The bone carries the heat to the inside more quickly.

42. For a juicier hamburger, add a little cold water to the beef before grilling.

43. To freeze meatballs, place them on a cookie sheet until frozen. Transfer to plastic bags and return to the freezer.

44. When boiling corn, add sugar to the water instead of salt. The salt will toughen the corn.

45. To ripen tomatoes, put them in a brown paper bag in a dark pantry.

46. To keep celery crisp, stand it upright in a pitcher of cold, salted water and refrigerate.

47. When cooking cabbage, place a small tin cup or can

half full of vinegar on the stove near the cabbage. It will absorb the odor.

48. Potatoes soaked in salt water for 20 minutes before baking will bake more rapidly.

49. Let raw potatoes stand in cold water for at least a half-hour before frying in order to improve the crispness of French-fried potatoes. Dry potatoes completely before adding to oil.

50. A few drops of lemon juice in the water will whiten boiled potatoes.

51. Buy mushrooms before they "open." When stems and caps are attached firmly, they are fresh.

52. Do not use metal bowls when mixing salads. Use wood or glass.

53. Lettuce keeps better if you store it in the refrigerator without washing it. Keep the leaves dry. Wash the lettuce before using.

54. Never use soda to keep vegetables green. It destroys the vitamin C.

55. If you over-salt your gravy, stir in some instant mashed potatoes to repair the damage. Add a little more liquid if necessary.

56. After stewing chicken, cool in broth before cutting to add more flavor.

COOKING TERMS

Au gratin: Topped with crumbs and/or cheese and browned in an oven or under a broiler.

Au jus: Served in its own juices.

Baste: To moisten foods during cooking with pan drippings or special sauce in order to add flavor and prevent drying.

Bisque: A thick cream soup.

Blanch: To immerse in rapidly boiling water and allow to cook slightly.

Cream: To soften a fat, like butter, by beating it at room temperature. Butter and sugar are often creamed together.

Crimp: To seal the edges of a two-crust pie either by pinching them at intervals with the fingers or a fork.

Crudités: An assortment of raw vegetables that is served as an hors d'oeuvre.

Degrease: To remove fat from the surface of stews and soups.

Dredge: To coat lightly with flour, cornmeal, bread crumbs, etc.

Entree: The main course.

Fold: To incorporate a delicate substance into another substance without releasing air bubbles.

Glaze: To cover with a glossy coating, such as a melted and diluted jelly for fruit desserts.

Julienne: To cut vegetables, fruits, or cheeses into match-shaped pieces.

Marinate: To allow food to stand in a liquid in order to tenderize or to add flavor.

Mince: To chop food into very small pieces.

Parboil: To boil until partially cooked; to blanch.

Pare: To remove the outer skin of a fruit or vegetable.

Poach: To cook gently in hot liquid kept just below the boiling point.

Saute: To cook food in a small amount of butter/oil.

Simmer: To cook in liquid just below the boiling point.

Steep: To let food stand in hot liquid in order to extract or enhance the flavor.

Toss: To combine ingredients with a repeated lifting motion.

Whip: To beat rapidly in order to incorporate air and produce expansion.

HERBS & SPICES

Basil: Sweet, warm flavor with an aromatic odor. Use whole or ground. Good with lamb, fish, roasts, stews, ground beef, vegetables, and dressings.

Bay Leaves: Pungent flavor. Use whole leaf but remove before serving. Good in vegetable dishes, seafood, stews and pickles.

Caraway: Spicy taste and aromatic smell. Use in cakes, breads, soups, cheese and sauerkraut.

Chives: Sweet, mild flavor like that of onion. Excellent in salads, fish, soups and potatoes.

Cilantro: Use fresh. Great in salads, salsa, fish, chicken, rice, beans and other Mexican dishes.

Curry Powder: Spices are combines to proper proportions to give a distinct flavor to meat, poultry, fish and vegetables.

Dill: Both seeds and leaves are flavorful. Leaves may be used as a garnish or cooked with fish, soup, dressings, potatoes, and beans. Leaves or the whole plant may be used to flavor pickles.

Fennel: Sweet, hot flavor. Both seeds and leaves are used. Use in small quantities in pies and baked goods. Leaves can be boiled with fish.

Ginger: A pungent root, this aromatic spice is sold fresh, dried, or ground. Use in pickles, preserves, cakes, cookies, and meat dishes.

Marjoram: May be used both dried or green. Use to flavor fish, poultry, omelets, lamb, stew, stuffing and tomato juice.

Mint: Aromatic with a cool flavor. Excellent in beverages, fish, lamb, cheese, soup, peas, carrots and fruit desserts.

Oregano: Strong and aromatic. Use whole or ground in tomato juice, fish, eggs, pizza, chili, poultry, vegetables.

Paprika: A bright red pepper, this spice is used in meat, vegetables and soups or as a garnish for potatoes, salads or eggs.

Parsley: Best when used fresh, but can be used dried. Try in fish, omelets, soup, meat and mixed greens.

Rosemary: Very aromatic. Can be used fresh or dried. Season fish, stuffing, beef, lamb, poultry, onions, and potatoes.

Saffron: Orange-yellow in color, this spice flavors or colors foods. Use in soup, chicken, rice and breads.

Sage: Use fresh or dried. The flowers are sometimes used in salads. May be used in fish, beef, poultry, cheese spreads and breads.

Tarragon: Leaves have a pungent, hot taste. Use to flavor sauces, salads, fish, poultry, tomatoes, eggs, green beans and dressings.

Thyme: Sprinkle leaves on fish or poultry before broiling or baking. Add a few sprigs directly on coals shortly before meat is finished grilling.

ARE YOUR HERBS & SPICES FRESH?

Ingredient Shelf Life:

- Ground Spices 2-3 years
- Whole Spices 3-4 years
- Seasoning Blends 1-2 years
- Herbs 1-3 years
- Extracts 4 years, except pure vanilla, which lasts forever

Still not sure, then use these guidelines:

- Check to see that the color of your spices and herbs is vibrant.

- If the color has faded, chances are so has the flavor.

- Rub or crush the spice or herb in your hand. If the aroma is weak and flavor is not apparent, it's time to replace it.

- Store herbs and spices in a tightly capped container, and keep away from heat, moisture, and direct sunlight. Replace bottle lids tightly immediately after use.

- To minimize moisture and caking, use a dry measuring spoon and avoid sprinkling directly into a steaming pot.

- Check the freshness date on the container.

GUIDELINES FOR BUYING FRESH VEGETABLES

Artichokes: Look for compact, tightly closed heads with green, clean-looking leaves. Avoid those with leaves that are brown or separated.

Asparagus: Stalks should be tender and firm; tips should be close and compact. Choose the stalks with very little white; they are more tender. Use asparagus soon after purchasing because it toughens rapidly.

Beans: Those with small seeds inside the pods are best. Avoid beans with dry-looking pods.

Broccoli, Brussels Sprouts, Cauliflower: Flower clusters on broccoli and cauliflower should be tight and close together. Brussels sprouts should be firm and compact. Smudgy, dirty spots may indicate pests or disease.

Cabbage and Head Lettuce: Choose heads that are heavy for their size. Avoid cabbage with worm holes and lettuce with discoloration or soft rot.

Cucumbers: Choose long, slender cucumbers for best quality. Avoid yellow ones.

Mushrooms: Caps should be closed around the stems. Avoid black or brown gills.

Peas and Lima Beans: Select pods that are well-filled but not bulging. Avoid dried, spotted, yellow, or flabby pods.

GUIDELINES FOR BUYING FRESH FRUITS

Bananas: Skin should be free of bruises and black or brown spots. Purchase green and allow them to ripen at home at room temperature.

Berries: Select plump, solid berries with good color. Avoid stained containers which indicate wet or leaky berries. Berries without clinging caps, such as blackberries and raspberries, may be unripe. Strawberries without caps may be overripe.

Melons: In cantaloupes, thick, close netting on the rind indicates best quality. Cantaloupes are ripe when the stem scar is smooth and the space between the netting is yellow or yellow-green. They are best when fully ripe with fruity odor. Honeydews are ripe when rind has creamy to yellowish color and velvety texture. Immature honeydews are whitish-green. Ripe watermelons have some yellow color on one side. If melons are white or pale green on one side, they are not ripe.

Oranges, Grapefruit and Lemons: Choose those heavy for their size. Smoother, thinner skins usually indicate more juice. Most skin markings do not affect quality. Oranges with a slight greenish tinge may be just as ripe as fully colored ones. Light or greenish-yellow lemons are more tart than deep yellow ones. Avoid citrus fruits showing withered, sunken or soft areas.

MEASUREMENTS

a pinch	1/8 teaspoon or less
3 teaspoons	1 tablespoon
4 tablespoons	1/4 cup
8 tablespoons	1/2 cup
12 tablespoons	3/4 cup
16 tablespoons	1 cup
2 cups	1 pint
4 cups	1 quart
4 quarts	1 gallon
8 quarts	1 peck
4 pecks	1 bushel
16 ounces	1 pound
32 ounces	1 quart
1 ounce liquid	2 tablespoons
8 ounces liquid	1 cup

Use standard measuring cups and spoons.

All measurements are level.

RECIPES BY CATEGORY

Salads

Side Dishes

Soups

Miscellaneous

TRADEMARKS

- Applebee's is a registered trademark of Applebee's International, Inc.
- A&W is a registered trademark of A&W Restaurants, Inc.
- B.B. King's Blues Club & Restaurant is a registered trademark of B.B. King Blues Club & Grill.
- Bahama Breeze is a registered trademark of Darden Concepts, Inc.
- Balducci's is a registered trademark of Balducci's.
- Bennigan's is a registered trademark of Bennigan's Grill & Tavern.
- Bisquick is a registered trademark of General Mills.
- Black-Eyed Pea is a registered trademark of Restaurants Acquisition 1, LLC.
- Bob Evans is a registered trademark of Bob Evans Farms Inc.
- Brown Derby is a registered trademark of The Brown Derby.
- California Pizza Kitchen is a registered trademark of California Pizza Kitchen, Inc.
- Carrabba's is a registered trademark of OSI Restaurant Partners, LLC.
- The Cheesecake Factory is a registered trademark of The Cheesecake Factory, Inc.
- Chi-Chi's is a registered trademark of Chi-Chi's, Inc. and Prandium, Inc.
- Chick-Fil-A is a registered trademark of CFA Properties, Inc.
- Chipotle Mexican Grill is a registered trademark of Chipotle Mexican Grill, Inc.
- Claim Jumper is registered trademark of Claim Jumper Restaurant LLC
- Cracker Barrel is a registered trademark of CBOCS Properties, Inc.
- Cracker Jack is a registered trademark of Frito-Lay North America, Inc.

- Dan Marino's is a registered trademark of LTP Management.
- Dave & Buster's is a registered trademark of Dave & Buster's.
- Denny's is a registered trademark of DFO, LLC.
- Dreamland is a registered trademark of Dreamland BBQ.
- El Torito is a registered trademark of El Torito Restaurants, Inc.
- Famous Dave's is a registered trademark of Famous Dave's of America, Inc.
- Four Seasons is a registered trademark of The Four Seasons Restaurant.
- Gardenburger is a registered trademark of Kellogs.
- Golden Corral is a registered trademark of Golden Corral Corporation.
- Hard Rock Café is a registered trademark of Hard Rock America, Inc.
- Houlihan's is a registered trademark of Houlihan's Restaurants, Inc.
- Howard Johnson's is a registered trademark of Howard Johnson International, Inc.
- In-N-Out is a registered trademark of In-N-Out Burger.
- Jack in the Box is a registered trademark of Jack In The Box Inc.
- Jimmy Buffett's Margaritaville Restaurant is a registered trademark of Margaritaville Cafe.
- Joe's Crab Shack is a registered trademark of Landry's Seafood Restaurants, Inc.
- Kenny Rogers Roasters is a registered trademark of Kenny Rogers Roasters.
- KFC, Pizza Hut,Taco Bell, and Long John Silver's are registered trademarks of Yum! Brands, Inc.
- Lawry's is a registered trademark of Lawry's Foods, LLC.
- Lipton's is a registered trademark of Unilever.

- Lone Star Steakhouse is a registered trademark of Lone Star.
- Macaroni Grill is a registered trademark of Brinker International.
- Mader's is a registered trademark of Mader's Restaurant.
- McDonald's and the Big Mac are trademarks of McDonald's Corporation.
- Mrs. Fields is a registered trademark of Mrs. Fields Gifts, Inc.
- Old Spaghetti Factory is a registered trademark of The Dussin Group.
- Olive Garden is a registered trademark of Darden Restaurants, Inc.
- Outback Steakhouse is a registered trademark of Outback Steakhouse, Inc.
- Pizzeria Uno is a registered trademark of Pizzeria Uno Corporation.
- P.F. Chang is a registered trademark of P.F. Chang's China Bistro, Inc.
- Red Lobster is a registered trademark of Darden Restaurants, Inc.
- Red Robin is a registered trademark of Red Robin International, Inc.
- Ritz Carlton is a registered trademark of The Ritz-Carlton Company, L.L.C.
- Ro-Tel is a registered trademark of ConAgra Foods, Inc.
- Ruby Tuesday is a registered trademark of Morrison Restaurants, Inc.
- Saks Fifth Avenue is a registered trademark of Saks Fifth Avenue.
- Sbarro is a registered trademark of Sbarro, Incorporated.
- Shoney's is a registered trademark of Shoney's, Inc.
- Sonic Drive-In is a registered trademark of America's Drive-In Brand Properties LLC.

- Subway is a registered trademark of Doctor's Associates Inc.
- Taco Bell is a registered trademark of Yum! Brands, Inc.
- Texas Roadhouse is a registered trademark of Texas Roadhouse, Inc.
- T.G.I. Friday's is a registered trademark of T.G.I. Friday's, Inc.
- Tony Roma's is a registered trademark of Tony Roma's, Inc.
- Trader Joe's is a registered trademark of Trader Joe's.
- V8 is a registered trademark of CSC Brands LP.
- Waldorf-Astoria is a registered trademark of Hilton.

To find a restaurant near you, please visit:

Applebee's	www.applebees.com
A&W	www.awrestaurants.com
B.B. King's Blues Club	www.bbkingblues.com
Bahama Breeze	www.bahamabreeze.com
Balducci's	www.balduccis.com
Benihana	www.benihana.com
Bennigan's	www.bennigans.com
Black-Eyed Pea	www.theblackeyedpea.com
Bob Evans	www.bobevans.com
Brown Derby	www.thehollywoodbrownderby.com
California Pizza Kitchen	www.cpk.com
Carrabba's Italian Grill	www.carrabbas.com
Cheesecake Factory	www.thecheesecakefactory.com
Chi-Chi's	www.chichis.com
Chick-Fil-A	www.chick-fil-a.com
Chipotle Mexican Grill	www.chipotle.com
Church's	www.churchs.com
Claim Jumper	www.claimjumper.com
Cracker Barrel	www.crackerbarrel.com
Dan Marono's	www.danmarinosrestaurant.com
Dave & Buster's	www.daveandbusters.com
Denny's	www.dennys.com
Dreamland BBQ	www.dreamlandbbq.com
El Torito	www.eltorito.com
Famous Dave's	www.famousdaves.com
Four Seasons	www.fourseasonsrestaurant.com
Golden Corral	www.goldencorral.com
Hard Rock Cafe	www.hardrockcafe.com
Houlihan's	www.houlihans.com
Howard Johnson	www.hojo.com
In-N-Out Burger	www.in-n-out.com
Jack in the Box	www.jackinthebox.com
Joe's Crab Shack	www.joescrabshack.com
Kenny Rogers Roasters	www.kennyrogers.cc
KFC	www.kfc.com
Lone Star Steakhouse	www.lonestarsteakhouse.com
Macaroni Grill	www.macaronigrill.com
Mader's	www.madersrestaurant.com
McDonald's	www.mcdonalds.com

Mrs. Field's	www.mrsfields.com
Old Spaghetti Factory	www.osf.com
Olive Garden	www.olivegarden.com
Outback Steakhouse	www.outback.com
P.F. Chang's	www.pfchangs.com
Pizzeria Uno	www.unos.com
Red Lobster	www.redlobster.com
Red Robin	www.redrobin.com
Ritz Carlton	www.ritzcarlton.com
Ruby Tuesday	www.rubytuesday.com
Saks Fifth Avenue	www.saksfifthavenue.com
Sbarro	www.sbarro.com
Shoney's	www.shoneys.com
Sonic Drive-In	www.sonicdrivein.com
Subway	www.subway.com
Taco Bell	www.tacobell.com
Texas Roadhouse	www.texasroadhouse.com
T.G.I. Friday's	www.fridays.com
Tony Roma's	www.tonyromas.com
Trader Joe's	www.traderjoes.com
Waldorf-Astoria	www.hilton.com/en/hi/waldorf

Recipe Favorites